In the Footsteps of the Few

To Live a Principled Life

By Craig D. Lounsbrough

God's best to you in all things.

For information, or to order additional copies, please contact:

Beacon Publishing Group
P.O. Box 41573 Charleston, S.C. 29423
800.817.8480| beaconpublishinggroup.com

Publisher's catalog available by request.

ISBN-13: 978-1-949472-43-1

ISBN-10: 1-949472-43-1

Published in 2022. New York, NY 10001.

First Edition. Printed in the USA.

In the Footsteps of the Few

To Live a Principled Life

Table of Contents

Dedication

My parents lived out what is outlined in the pages of this book. Had they not done so, this book would not exist. Many people talk about living out a principled life, as they talk about doing many things. However, as the old saying goes, "talk is cheap." My parents didn't talk. They acted.

I've found that it's rather easy to live out these principles when the winds are favorable, the tides are gentle, and the skies of life remain blue and rubbed warm. But when life turns dark and you're pounded by the gale force winds of adversity, things are different. It is in such a maelstrom that the power of these principles is either shown to be steadfast or they fall fast. Having had a front-row seat to principle and integrity walking the hard road of life through the life of my parents, I came to understand the renewing essence, the raw power, and the uncompromising necessity of such living. Therefore, this book is dedicated to Mom and Dad. Thank you for your timeless and Christ-centered example that convinced me of the power of these principles.

This book is also dedicated to my children. I have watched both of them sort through life in their efforts to determine what is important verses what is said to be important. I have stood at their sides and watched them grapple with choices large and small. And in the end, I have watched them make the choices that will serve them well while many of those around them did not. Therefore, this book is dedicated to Cheyenne and

Corey. Thanks to both of you for allowing me the privilege of observing two young hearts navigate the many choices offered up by a world spiraling down. You have both done marvelously well.

Likewise, my thanks to Beacon Publishing Group for their untiring assistance in bringing this book from the platform of my laptop to the reality of print. Your support, professionalism, and undying efforts are deeply appreciated.

Finally, but foremost, I want to thank God that I have been repeatedly granted the priceless privilege of watching hardy souls as they braced themselves against the winds of all kinds of adversities, only to hold onto that which is good and true despite the ferocity of those winds. Your examples have been deeply profound, enduring in their inspiration, and perpetually life-altering.

Introduction

"I love your books," she said. Hers was a voice that I hadn't heard for somewhere over five years. Who she was is irrelevant to the story. Her timing was not.

I had wrestled for over a year whether or not to write this book. There was something of a brisk energy borne of a compelling sort of passion that drove my other books. However, for this one, that passion was missing. Despite my forced efforts to cultivate that passion or somehow search it out, I could only grasp the barest edge of it, and then only for a moment. And so, sitting void of what had driven my other books, I asked if the absence of this passion was a sign that this book was not to be.

I prayed for a sign of any kind; some sort of revelation despite how small that would direct me either way. I knew the material. I was aware of the thesis of the book and how I would shape it. I believed that such a book was potently and pointedly relevant for the nature and contour of our times, particularly today. I believed that God gave me the experiences out which to write it with poignancy, and the wordsmithing skills to robustly deliver it. But that unique passion that drives an artist to the edges of his talent and beyond was missing and I could not recapture it.

The prayers came back unanswered. The months rolled into a year and then some. I pressed God again and again with some degree of escalating frustration, consuming myself with other worthy projects. The feeling that I was looking for never came, but the phone call did.

"I love your books," she said. "They've meant so much to me." And without any pause in her voice at all, the final question, "Have you written anymore?"

There are those times when God speaks, but in the speaking you realize that in your own head you have scripted a very tightly predetermined answer. And that answer becomes so tightly predetermined that any other answer is missed. We lead such horribly scripted lives that the voice of God and the majesty of His movements that give substance to that voice are not heard because they don't fit the script. We become deaf by our own design.

I was looking for passion. My singular criteria as to whether I was to write this book or not sat squarely and immovably upon my demand that this slightly smoking ember had to be fanned into an unquenchable flame. That passion would arise stalwart and irrefutable, subsequently thrusting me forward with its robustness and energy. But that phone call did not deliver that passion. At all.

What I failed to see is that to write a book of this nature, the absence of passion but the presence of conviction would make the task inordinately harder, but the product infinitely richer. That maybe the richness of this book arose out of the energy drawn from nothing other than raw conviction. That this raw conviction absent of passion helps us to somehow sort through the pablum and cast out the fluff in order to speak with the rawness that is required to transform hearts and change nations. That while many might see conviction and passion as the same, the greatest words arise out of our weakest moments. The call came. The passion did not, but the conviction did. My rubric shifted. And that evening I began to write.

This book is about ascending the heights of virtue and walking the arduous road of integrity, both of which have been forsaken by much of our culture. It is about being bold when others are not. It extols the challenge that we need to embrace the principles scorned by others but blessed by God. It was written out of the core conviction born out of spending the bulk of my day sitting on the front row of a deteriorating culture and feeling utterly remiss in not speaking something into the deterioration.

And while this book is written to confront a sinful and decadent culture, such a singular orientation would be far too short-sighted. In many ways, the need to confront our culture is eclipsed by a compelling sense that we are much more than what we've become. What we see is not who we are. What we've done is not what we're capable of. Rather, it is who we have chosen to be and what we have chosen to do. And our choices are saddening.

This book is not about what we've become and what we have done, although it certainly confronts such choices. Rather, it's about who we can become and the good that we can do. It's about courageous living based on ethical choices that elevate us to places we thought untouchable. It's about reversing the descending fall of our lives by intentionally ascending the state of our souls. It embodies a deep hope and a relentless conviction that the summit is ours for the taking, and the road is in fact the very journey that we were born for. It is about igniting the fullness of our humanity instead of feeding slop to our darker side. It is about a transformation that likely few will make. But it only takes a few to change many.

I am grateful for unexpected phone calls and for a God who lavishes His grace upon us even when we're looking elsewhere. And I am thankful that conviction is strong enough to propel us even when passion has fallen to the fatigue involved in saving a culture. May the words penned, and the concepts shared transform you in ways either large or small. And should they achieve that rather formidable task, the energy expended will have been more than worth it.

Chapter One
What I Want
The Frightening Call of Great Things

"So Eli told Samuel, 'Go and lie down, and if he calls you, say, 'Speak, LORD, for your servant is listening.' So Samuel went and lay down in his place. The LORD came and stood there, calling as at the other times, 'Samuel! Samuel!' Then Samuel said, 'Speak, for your servant is listening.'"

- 1 Samuel 3:9-10 (NIV)

"Let us always remember that Christ calls men and women not only to trust Him as Savior, but also to follow Him as Lord. That call to discipleship must be part of our message if we are to be faithful to Him."

- Billy Graham

I want to be happy, but I don't think I want to be satisfied; for satisfaction lures me into believing that happiness is found in reaching some point rather than realizing happiness is born of striving for those points. I want to experience a resilient and wonderfully endearing sense of contentment that neatly threads itself through every part of my soul, but I don't want that contentment to morph into the baser mentality of complacency. I want to keep a weathered eye on every horizon, but I want to do more than just watch those horizons from some sorry distance. Rather, I want to walk their ridges. I don't want to contemplate the taking of a journey. Rather, I want to be contemplating a journey as I'm taking it.

I want to robustly celebrate the achievements and vigorously revel in the milestones in a manner completely worthy of them, but I never want to fall to the bane of mediocrity that would prompt me to see them as a terminus. I want to develop a sturdy confidence born of the advances made, and I want to have that confidence perpetually reinforced by the successes achieved. Yet, I pray that my failures will always serve to temper that confidence so that it never turns to rot in the form of arrogance. And in further managing this tempered confidence, I never want it to be so strong that I errantly assume any challenge as too small to be worthy of my time. I want to be happy, but I don't think I want to be satisfied.

For whatever reason I might do it and in whatever way I might do it, I never want to hand myself excuses to round the next summit instead of scaling it. I never want to slothfully presume the ability to achieve a goal without holding myself accountable to actually getting on the track and running the race. And I suppose worst of all, I never want to scan my assorted array of trophies, whether they be numerous or few, and in the scanning embrace some languid sense born of complacency that somehow it is done and that I can hang up my hat, when in reality life is never done and no hat is really ever hung.

Why Do I 'Never Want' to Do These Things?

Laziness is humanity domesticated to its own destruction. Mediocrity is life pent up in the very ironclad cages that we create out of the misguided notion that an 'adventure' is a product of those misty-eyed idealists who expend their lives chasing dreams too elusive to catch. Therefore, we create dreams that we can cage so that they simply can't elude us, and in their captivity we can manage them so that, God forbid, they never manage us. And what we forget is that a dream caged is nothing more than an anemic, pasty-white wish that is always in the process of dying in whatever cage it happens to find itself.

We Are Made for More

We are made for more than all of that. Our humanity yearns for the next adventure. We desire lofty summits and distant finish lines that tax the whole of our energies in order to get us to them. There is inherent within us this incessant sense that where 'we are' is not where 'we're going,' and that to park it wherever we're at is to start dying in that very place. There is some fixed notion in our psyche and some insistent voice in our souls that will not be silenced and cannot be appeased by lesser agendas. These call out despite the many ways we work to silence them, and in the calling out they call us out.

Sadly, in light of the calling, we too often surrender to fear and we sell-out to apathy. We foolishly peddle our resources and pawn off our talents to lesser things so that we can hold up some small, pithy achievement to offset the gnawing guilt we experience over bypassing the greater achievements that were our calling before we were called away. We can't show up empty-handed, for that would work against our efforts to squelch the already suppressed voice of passion. Yet, unless we set our sights on higher things we will always be empty-hearted, for blind obedience to fear and the steady ingestion of apathy leaves everything it touches empty. And I would propose that emptiness of this sort is the bedfellow of death itself.

Therefore, we achieve something because we must. And at times we dress up those 'somethings' so that they don't look half bad. But too often our achievements are an insidious effort to sedate our sense of passion and render it appeased. They're the anemic manifestation of our fears, a groveling by-product of our lackluster vision, and a response to the snide voice of mediocrity that herald's 'passion' as the fool's errand.

Passion is not fooled, even though we are fooled by the belief that we somehow fooled it. To numb passion is not to diminish its power. Rather, it is to diminish our sense of its power. In doing so we stepped down instead of stepping up. We swapped mountains for back alleys, and dramatic vistas for fading fences. And these realities create a grinding angst within us that will not be soothed by anything but heeding the call from which we've run.

What to Do?
Decide to Do Something

As obvious as it may sound, the first thing to do is decide to do something. Without the decision to do something, anything and everything is only an idea. An idea, regardless of how ingenious or bold changes nothing until it is birthed as a reality. The greatest ideas will only tickle our imagination, but they won't fire it until they're released. They will nudge us, but they won't force us to jump. They will call, but they won't beg.

To do something is to decide to be disciplined. It's a decision to take a step rather than toy with ideas. It is a choice to move from the non-committal ease of playing out various scenarios in our head, to grabbing one of them by the throat and acting on it. It is not based on cost in stepping out, for the greatest cost of all is in not stepping out. And it is the sad reality that most of our ideas die without ever having been birthed as realities because we choose to do everything but step.

Decide If You're Going to be Brave

An idea as only an 'idea' and nothing more than an idea is safe. As ideas and ideas only, they're manageable. They're domesticated. They're leashed. We hold them within the safe confines of our minds and our imaginations, toying with them as time permits and returning them to those confines when it does not. But cut the reigns and turn an idea loose and it may not be as manageable and domesticated as we might like it to be. So, are we brave enough for the ride that is certain to ensue?

An idea that is given legs is one of the most dangerous things imaginable, but it is also one of the most exciting things possible. An idea running at full stride is wildly frightening in a manner that unleashes something that was never supposed to be leashed. It is not about throwing caution to the wind as some might think. Rather, it's about stepping into the wind and being swept up by it while wisely holding caution as we do. It's about understanding that wisdom is not held hostage to safety. Rather, wisdom is based on figuring out how we navigate dangerous things in a way that no longer renders them dangerous. And as such, are we going to choose to be brave?

Decide How Important Comfort and Familiarity Are

Unleash your ideas and things will never be the same; guaranteed. Things will change when great ideas are unleashed because they can't help but change. What 'is' will become the stuff of a history that will lay beyond our ability to ever reclaim again. Our ideas are the stuff of the future. They are never home in the present for the present is only the thing that launches them, not the thing that cultivates them. If our lives have been expended in the acquisition of comfort and the cultivation of familiarity, our future is our 'now' and no idea can sufficiently grow in that.

While the degree of success rests on the magnitude of the idea being released, the greater degree to which it will be successful is the degree to which we unleash it. And if we prefer familiarity and the comfort that it engenders, we might never truly let an idea loose, or we may well attempt to cram it back into the confines we released it from after we've unleashed it. At best, the ideas are hamstrung. At worst, they perish.

Get the Resources

If you've decided that you want to do something, if you're sufficiently brave to do it, and if you're willing to forgo familiarity and comfort in the pursuit of it, then get the resources that you need to make it happen. Real resources. This is not about thin and pasty resources, nor is it about material that's been worn thin. It's not about sugary-sweet notions or trite sayings that are fun and fanciful but are shallow and porous.

Rather, this is about finding bold, honest, timely, daring, frank, deep and brisk material that will thrust you out beyond the confines you saw as the terminus of your dreams. Find resources that are unforgiving in helping you grow, reliable in content, proven in substance, and thick with wisdom. Learn from trusted people who have been there-and-back who have likewise taken other people there-and-back. Grab these resources, let them grab you, and then rigorously apply them without delay or excuse. When you do, you will start the process of placing yourself in a position to begin heeding the call of great things.

Chapter Two
Not Where We Were
Finding Ourselves Somewhere Else

"I have strayed like a lost sheep. Seek your servant, for I have not forgotten your commands."

- Psalm 119:176 (NIV)

"I've never been lost, but I was mighty turned around for three days once."

- Daniel Boone

It seems that we have some vague and rather ethereal sense of where we're going in this thing called life. For the more contemplative soul, that sense might be quite refined. For the casual traveler, it might be a bit more nebulous and scattered. For many, where they're going is defined by the tasks of the day, rather than enlarged by a vision for tomorrow.

In many cases where we're going is far more rigorously defined by all the places where we don't want to go, rather than the places where we do want to go. At other times its definition is rather handily shaped by the opinions of others, or it's carved directly from the bedrock of the value systems that have been built into our lives throughout the whole of our lives. For others, it's based on the need to avoid the pain of our past or somehow prove our worth in the face of a self-image that lays battered and bloodied. Vague or refined, we all have some sense of where we're going.

And too often, we find ourselves ending up someplace else.

Some of us are not necessarily in conscious pursuit of wherever this place is. We have this instinctually primal sense that it's there and we intuitively assume that our path will take a natural course to wherever that place is. Then, there are others of us who are myopically focused on where we're going to the degree that everything that we do is wholly defined by that singularly beguiling destination. Some of the more adventurous souls among us nimbly pursue that destination, spiritedly pulling in as much of everything that we can along the way to accentuate both the journey as well as the destination. In whatever way we do it, we all have some sense of where we're going. And too often, we find ourselves ending up someplace else.

The Detours We Create

Yet, life is not so predictable as to always wind its way to the places that we presumed it to be going. There are those times when where we were going was bafflingly mistaken as some sort of final destination when in reality it was only a step to a final destination. At other times the place where we're going is really a destination that we had fabricated because the place to which life had originally called us appeared too big, or too far, or too steep, or simply impossible in whatever way our limited vision happened to interpret it. At such times we craft some other less intimidating and thoroughly unfulfilling destination. Sometimes our destination is to set a course away from our destination so that we can dispense with whatever responsibility or obligation our original destination might have demanded of us.

And then in the magic of life, there are those times where we have actually pursued some authentic destination with such rigorous tenacity that the trajectory of our efforts has catapulted us past our destination to places that are everything of our furthest and fondest imagination. However, it might play out, we're all headed somewhere.

The Detours Life Creates

But then there are those other times when life takes a sharp turn that seems little of our actions, nothing of our destination, but everything of circumstances designed to kill our journey and crush our destination long before we get within arm's length of it. There's a sense that something intrinsically unjust, stealthy and evil is always about and on the prowl, and whatever it is, it's bound to show up if it hasn't already. When it does, it undoes everything that we thought was secure and certain, wreaking havoc on whatever our journey had been to that point. And to whatever degree it wrecks the road underneath our feet, we're left in a blurring trauma that renders our journey disjointed, our destination uncertain, and our lives dispirited.

The Explanation of Detours Missed
How It Happens

Yet, more often than not it's the not the obvious shifts in our journey that are the core problem. Sure, life shows up and we get shoved down. There's no question that the natural ebb and flow of life, whether it be titanic or miniscule, will happen to us. Despite our frequently ego-centric inclinations to the contrary, we are not so shrewd or ingenious as to be able to traverse life in a manner that deftly side-steps everything that comes at us. We don't dance as well as we think we do. Our ingenuity falls prey to our arrogance, and the winds that we assumed to be reliable often shift and drive our genius toward some rocky shoal. And so, life will fall upon us, or ram against us, or pull the ground out from under us, or wreck us.

Casual and Careless

Yet, more often than not, the explanation doesn't rest in life having shown up. The much more poignant issue is that too often we are passive, flabby and lax in rigorously living out our lives. We're far too casual and careless. Somehow, somewhere the exquisite sanctity of life and the priceless privilege of living it out was supplanted with some sense that it's too much work or that it's not going to work, so why try? The gift is lost in the grind and we lose a sustaining sense of gratitude.

We get caught in the shallows, forgetting that the deepest waters hold the greatest treasures. But we would rather forage for trinkets because treasures are too stubborn to just hand themselves to us and we will not succumb to such preposterous demands. The shallows become our calling when they are nothing more than our coffin. Therefore, we drift without knowing that we're drifting because we're no longer paying attention. We come to believe that we are living a life of great things because it is too overwhelming to embrace the truth that we have forfeited great things. The outcome of such passive living is that we end up finding ourselves somewhere else without ever seeing it coming.

Preoccupied with Pabulum

Too often we're too preoccupied with pabulum. We're tediously engaged with tiny things and we're caught in the tedium of minutia because we can gather these things around us and control them when the bigger things are out of our control. Too frequently we're goaded by the fear of big dreams and massive possibilities, so we dumb down our lives to anesthetize those fears.

There's plenty of pablum to go around. Therefore, we assume that if we collect sufficient quantities of it, it will add up to something bigger than pablum. Yet, dreams are never constructed of pablum and our fears are never put at bay by any collection of it, regardless of how massive. It is an escape, but it is never an answer. It's a detour, but it is never a destination. It is an imitation of what we are attempting to avoid. Subsequently, pablum gives us a sense that we can circumvent everything that we fear and still achieve everything that we dream. We're caught in small things, and the outcome is that we end up finding ourselves somewhere else without ever seeing it coming.

Along for the Ride

Frequently we presume that we're some docile passenger along for a ride that's going wherever it's going, so we just let it go to wherever that place is. We freely surrender to passivity which is an invitation to meaninglessness. And meaninglessness is the death of the soul itself. Life is a river, we say. And the best course of action is to navigate it because entertaining the far-fetched notion of swimming against it is utterly preposterous.

Assuming that we are along for the ride releases us from any accountability for the ride and where it might end up. We are innocent. Or we're victims of circumstance. Or our families put us here because they didn't know any other place to put us. Or we're simply being obedient to whatever we've subjected ourselves to. Assuming we're on a ride that we can't direct, the outcome is that we end up finding ourselves somewhere else without ever seeing it coming.

The Walls of Denial

At other times, we live in the constructed confines erected from the raw material of denial, causing us to live out a life that is in denial of life itself. We become squatters living in a squatter's camp constructed by the flimsy materials of justification, rationalization, blame-placing and projecting. We pull in the walls due to the reality that materials of this sort are always pulling inward because they will die if we dare to press them outward. Hemmed in by walls of this sort, the world around us is shut out and moves on without our awareness of it.

We live in walls that we pretend are horizons, or vast doorways that open to massive expanses and marvelous places. In time, we come to believe that they are not walls at all as we've visualized them as something that they will never be. We then live out our lives in these confining hovels, convinced that we are forging great mountains and running in wild places. The outcome is that we end up finding ourselves somewhere else without ever seeing it coming.

Ending Up Where We Wish to Be

We will end up somewhere. The fact that we have a destination is irrefutable as life is a journey that presents us with no option other than the journey. We may decide that the nature and course of the journey is irrelevant, and we may take a backseat to passivity. If we do, we have no right to complain when we end up in some place other than what we may have thought or preferred.

Yet, we can recognize that we are not automatons subject to the flux of the world within which we have found ourselves. It would seem advisable to recognize that we have an obligation to the course that our life is taking, and that along with that obligation we have been granted a profound degree of power to bring to the course. If we imprudently succumb to carelessness, or become engrossed by pabulum, or if we just let the ride go wherever circumstances take it, or if we pull close the walls of denial this thing that we call life will wind itself to wherever it's going with no one at the helm. And that kind of destination cannot be good.

We would be wise to inventory our lives and determine if we are in some way large or small participating in any of these behaviors. If so, we need to root them out and expunge them from our lives. Reclaiming a sense of vision, and then seizing our lives with discipline and intentionality will set us on a path that will land us in places that we've dreamt to land. If we don't, the place we land may not be on any land that we even remotely recognize.

Chapter Three
To Believe in Something Better
The Rise Against 'What Is'

"Jesus looked at them and said, "With man this is impossible, but with God all things are possible."
- Matthew19:26 (NIV)

"Nothing is impossible to a willing heart."
- John Heywood

Our humanity is ingeniously fashioned in a manner that it can handily break the realities that would seek to break it. Our existence need never be held hostage nor pressed into servitude to the sordid realities of all that is happening around us. Rather, we are able to stand in spirited opposition to those realities, and in the face of them we are capable of crafting brilliant and utterly resilient solutions that crush those realities by transforming them. We are dreamers and the authors of visions. We have the ability to conceptualize marvelous things and actually begin the act of crafting them even at those times when the presence of them or the hope for them is entirely non-existent. We are a powerful bunch vested with immense potential that exceeds even that which we understand.

Yet, we bring these abilities to bear against a world that would wish to press us flat in its skepticism. The world becomes embroiled in the selfish pursuits that it crafts as it chases things born of greed, gluttony and selfishness. The world would bend us to its darker ways rather than be bent to a better way. The world would prefer to kill both us and itself rather than give up what it has selfishly given itself over to. Indeed, the world has sold its soul to something that it is convinced will liberate the soul that it sold. Therefore, in the insanity of a world gone rogue, the world will viciously fight for the things that are certain to destroy it.

The weight of living in a world such as this, as well as the incessant press of darkness that such living spawns can at times leave us wondering if our influence might be too insufficient to wrestle the world out of a darkness that has become so terribly dark. We stand as single entities, bringing what light we can. Most times, that light seems swallowed in the vast darkness that seems to advance without restraint. We are left in the squalor of a battle that seems lost, only holding the line so that we can delay the full descent of evil and grant ourselves a few precious moments before life is over.

To Believe In Something Better

But we forget. We are extraordinarily quick to lose touch with a greater reality that infinitely surpasses the darkness which surrounds us. Our perspective becomes one of gradual defeat and continual hopelessness. Our understanding of who we are and Who we serve is lost in the grief of a battle seemingly hopeless and ground perpetually surrendered. We fall prey to the lies of the darkness whose own darkness is completely dependent upon our fear of it. Therefore, the darkness must appear dark beyond what it is in order to create the fear necessary to insure its own survival. It is not an undefeatable foe. It is, in fact, a foe that fears lest we discover the power that we possess and the vulnerability that it has.

Therefore, to remind us of who we are in times such as these and to fan the flames of our passion, I have compiled a number of quotes that I have had the privilege of authoring. It is my desire to call us back to lofty dreams and rigorous passion. To remind us that the darkness is the absence of light and therefore is totally dependent on the light remaining absent. As such, the darkness is terribly vulnerable as it possesses no means by which to stop the light other than creating fear in us. These quotes are written to set us free and send us out in the marvel of our humanity to change a world that is too ill-equipped to change itself. To say that we stand for something better, and that we will be that 'something better' in the standing. It is my hope that these quotes will move you to move your world, for I believe that you can, and I believe that you will:

The Rise Against 'What Is'

"If it didn't go all that well today, tomorrow is the opportunity that I have to do what I did today without doing it the way that I did it today."

"Pull every dream that you've ever had from all of the places that you've abandoned them, brush them off, set them in front of yourself, run the fingers of your heart over each of them, fight the lie that you're not enough to achieve them, and realize that the dream was not too big. Rather, the belief in yourself is too small."

"Let us not fall prey to the leaching negativity and rank pessimism that runs unleashed all around us. Rather, with the utmost determination we must bring ourselves to understand that these lies have been given legitimacy by people who thought themselves as powerless in the face of them, rather than recognizing that we have the power to rip the face off of them."

"You, yes you are the impossible waiting to happen. And the only reason that that sounds impossible to you is that you haven't been daring enough to push the possible out to the point where it becomes what you once mistook for the impossible."

"I am begging you to let nothing shackle you that God has sent you to unshackle."

"I've sat with tens of thousands of people and I've stared into as many empty eyes. And I must say that the inexplicable contradiction for me is that despite the gaping emptiness engulfing every one of these eyes, there yet lies within each one a wonderfully formidable gifting, an irrepressible energy, a depth yet undiscovered, riches unfathomed, and the resources to amply transform this ever-darkening world. And I've seen enough eyes to know that if yours are also empty, like everyone else's they are also full."

"God doesn't ask if something can be done. Nor does He ask if we have the resources to do it. For God is bound by neither question. And when we stand with God, neither are we."

"You are fully and magnificently equipped to stand up and change the world around you. And to simply sit down and tolerate the world around you is to squander who you are in the process of never being who you are."

"Do not be ashamed of who you are, for in doing so you are not taking into account the majesty of all that you are. And without any shred of doubt, I know that you are a person of majesty, for in my innumerable years of working with people I have yet to find even one person who is not."

"Stand up and be the light that God created you to be. Stand with me and the millions of others like both of us who have bowed before this inexplicably marvelous God of ours and in the bowing have begged that He not let us die until the darkness in the world around us has died first."

"Look in the mirror. Go ahead and look yet again. And look not at the reflection, for while this body of yours is marvelously complex in ways that continue to elude the reach of modern science, it is but a simple shell that holds the image of God within you. And if the shell is that grand, how much more what God has placed inside of it."

"If I let that which I hold to be true fall victim to a world that says it is not, I have in that action surrendered to the voices of those who know nothing of the truth other than to destroy it because it terrifies them. And if there's one thing I should be terrified of, it's not the surrender itself, but the fact that in the surrender I have given the world permission to avoid the very thing that it should fear."

"It's not the gifts or the abilities or the talents that equip us to accomplish great things. Rather, it's the persistent and adamantly stubborn conviction that we will in no way leave the world the way that we found it. And I would rather join hands with a single person of this kind than sit with a million gifted people who are not of this kind."

And finally…

"I will spend my life believing in you so that you will someday commit to doing the same."

To Believe

We must press ourselves into a sort of reckoning. We must realign our minds with the truth of who we are, who God created us to be, and the fantastic mission that He gifted us with. In a battle this pervasive and insidious, we must ground ourselves in a truth so brilliant and pristinely clean that it will handily stand against the wiles of the devil and the depth of the darkness he has spun. We must align ourselves with a reality so brilliant, robust and muscular that we find ourselves unintimidated by the darkness that now stands quaking in front of us.

We have a God who has called us to great things. Great things. He has not called us to defeat or even some slightly marginal victory. He has called us to complete and unquestioned victory. And such a call would never have been extended had not this God of ours provided ample resources to achieve that victory.

Before moving to the next chapter, I would encourage you to reread the quotes shared in this chapter. I would likewise encourage you to pick one that speaks to you, to write it down, and recite it daily. Let its truth seep deep into your soul and ignite your heart. Let it breath confidence into your spirit and energy into your convictions. Indeed, it is time to rise against 'what is.' So, let's rise.

Chapter Four
I Was Thinking
To Think Outside the Box(s)

"However, as it is written: 'What no eye has seen, what no ear has heard, and what no human mind has conceived' -- the things God has prepared for those who love him— "

I Corinthians 2:9 (NIV)

"Every child is an artist. The problem is how to remain an artist once we grow up."

Pablo Picasso

I was thinking. And the more I thought, the more I realized that there is a whole lot to think about. But in my thinking, I thought that most of our thinking (despite how much there is to think about) is really pretty standardized and chafingly rote. We think in predetermined patterns and pre-existent templates that require no thinking, other than the commitment not to think. We think in the way that others have chosen to think because they've already done the thinking, which relieves us of the need to do so. We think we think, but the more I think about that, the less I think we think (if you know what I mean). So, while there's a whole lot to think about in this big, wide world of ours …we don't.

It seems that our thinking is constrained in a manner

that there's really not that much thinking going on at all. Rather, more often than not our thinking is a tired process of monotonously gathering up a predictable handful of stale but safe thoughts. And if we play with them long enough, we figure that maybe they'll freshen up and something innovatively fragrant might actually emerge out of the rot. If something actually does, we're usually scared of whatever it is. If it doesn't (which is typically what happens) we become increasingly convinced beyond hope that life is actually as stale as we thought it was.

Why?

Most of this appears to happen because we think within boxes that we randomly (and sometimes not so randomly) borrow. We think within predetermined boxes because anything outside of those requires some innovation wherein we let the leash out a bit, let our thoughts find their legs, and let them run. But we've discovered that sometimes that simply takes too much thought, far too much energy, and far, far too much courage, for it is much easier and much, much safer to just sit. Or worse yet, we fear that once our thoughts have caught even the slightest whiff of a life running at full stride, they will forever refuse the short leash.

What if our thinking were to open up fresh venues and pull back some hitherto hidden veil that suddenly revealed vast horizons that leaves ignorance no place to hide? And what if the magnitude of such revelations is such that it handily crushes the complacency within which we've found so much comfort? What if? And out of the fear that such things might actually befall us, we peruse the stank back alleys of complacency, hastily borrowing boxes that we find deep in the darkened hovels of mediocrity. And life becomes a journey lived within suffocating boxes rather than an adventure crafted of breathless horizons.

Our Box Collection:
The Box of Societal Norms

We think within the box of societal norms. We grant these norms legitimacy because most of the people around us adhere to them in one form or another. Because all these people adhere to them, we naturally grant these norms a morality, assuming that others would not dare embrace them if they weren't sufficiently ethical or moral. Therefore, (despite the terribly narrow nature of both the boxes and our logic), they are deemed acceptable. To our relief, we quickly discover that if we think within these boxes we are far less likely to be met with rejection, or ridicule, or disdainful judgement, or some other rather distasteful response. We desperately want to be in the good graces of those around us as that's far more comfortable and far less dangerous than being in some other more adverse state of relationship with these people. Therefore, the rules of the box rule out the role of thinking.

The Box of the Mundane

We think within the well-worn boxes of the mundane as that path is quite well charted, rigorously predictable, and therefore void of anything dangerous because other people have figured out where all the dangerous stuff is and either removed it, or they've created paths around it. We know that venturing off the path in life is ref with all sorts of calamity that's just waiting to happen, and so in the box of the mundane there's nothing to venture off on because there's one and only one path. It might be mundane, it might go nowhere, but it's safe (if you happen to define 'safe' as refusing to live in order to effectively avoid being hurt). In an increasingly busy world that's careening in every conceivable direction, the box of the mundane allows us to perfectly function on autopilot since there's only one path that we can walk. Better yet, if we so choose we can simply sit along the side of this singular path, as this box generously allows us to somehow think (because we're not) that sitting is a journey. Therefore, the rules of the box rule out the role of thinking.

The Box of Our Fears

We think within the box of our fears, as anything on the outside of those walls is filled with horrific danger (often of the most fabricated sort). We've probably ventured out there a time or two, and when we did, we got hurt. And so, when we were hurt, we put our pain on emotional steroids which exponentially magnified our fear. We then took that fear and fashioned a monster that doesn't exist, and we hunkered down in our box horrified by the fiction of it all. And while the space out there is a whole lot bigger than the infinitesimally tiny space in here, at least it's safe. And safety (in our minds) is a decent trade-off, so much so that we amply decorate the box and make it homey with the scant furnishings of justification, rationalization, denial and other carefully appointed excuses. We settle into the scantily upholstered armchair of mediocrity and wile away our days pretending that we're not pretending. Therefore, the rules of the box rule out the role of thinking.

The Box of Our Families

We think within the box created by our families as we engaged them growing up. In many unhealthy families, their boxes were shaped by their own demons and assorted hobgoblins that they handed the reins of power over to. Over time, they dutifully passed those onto us lock, stock and barrel. Sometimes these families demand that family members stay within those boxes because, somehow, we will vanish into the dank darkness of another life, or be whisked off to parts unknown by friends, or fall headlong into a career if we dare step outside of them. Other times, family members may prompt us to move outside of the box because they have come to recognize the life-sucking quality of the box. Yet, while they prompt us to step out, they did not know how to do so themselves. Therefore, we must do the most daring thing imaginable and think through exactly how in the world we're going to do that. Therefore, the rules of the box rule out the role of thinking.

The Box of Self-Esteem

We think within the box crafted by our low self-esteems. These are often the smallest of all boxes because we dare not create any room whatsoever for anyone else to come in lest they see how pathetically awful we really are. Sitting in our confining hovel, we know full well that there's great adventure and untapped possibilities outside of our boxes. There's a good chance that we studied it, or read about it, or on those better days taken a slight peek outside before slamming the door shut again. In fact, knowing all of that is often the most difficult thing of all. We know outside this box of ours there's more life than we can wrap our solitary minds around. We constantly hear the invitations to come out. We can imagine adventure because we've imagined it so many times that we can almost touch it in our minds, which makes us think that somehow we're touching the adventure out there (which in fact, we are not). But we doubt our ability to function in it, or find a place in it, or seize it in the cultivation of our dreams, or much less survive it. Therefore, the rules of the box rule out the role of thinking.

I Was Thinking

I was thinking that there are a whole lot of boxes. Lots and lots of them. But I was also thinking that they are just boxes and nothing more. A box is not a fortified prison with towering walls and tangled barbwire, even though we have come to see it as such. It's just a box and nothing more. And as a box, it doesn't hold us. Rather, we hold it. I don't 'think' that we have the power to move beyond our boxes. Rather, I 'know' that we do. And when we realize that power and move beyond our boxes, the parameters of our lives will explode exponentially in a manner that we will be free to think about all the many things that this big, wide world of ours has to think about. When we do, the role of thinking will finally destroy the rules of the box. And when that happens, we will be genuinely free. And when we're free we won't be imprisoned by the dark specter of endings. Rather, we can embrace the majesty of our purpose, and we can run with the power of our calling.

And so, I think I really, really want to think outside the boxes. So, I think I'll start getting rid of them. It might take some time. I'm going to have to be honest about them and grieve what they've already stolen from me. It might be scary (in fact, I know it will be). I may wonder what in the world I'm doing at times. People may wonder what I'm doing as they peer out from the cracks in their own boxes. But to not get rid of the boxes is to rot away in a box. And I know that that is not the life for me. And might I say, I don't think that's the life for you either. So, let's begin the process of letting the role of thinking destroy the rules of the box. And let's be free.

Chapter Five
Am I Paying Attention?
Being Vigilant

"Be alert and of sober mind. Your enemy the devil prowls around like a roaring lion looking for someone to devour."

- I Peter 5:8 (NIV)

"Too much looking can get in the way of seeing".

- Patrick Rothfuss

A question that we need to ask if we're going to live a robust life is, "Are we paying attention?" Are we paying attention to the fact that we're probably not paying attention? Or more pointedly, can we actually pay attention to the fact that we're not paying attention, and can we come to understand that we're not paying attention because we're paying attention to the fear that keeps us from paying attention? Are we paying attention?

We're moving, but it's likely that we're moving within the current of the larger culture, or the dictating demands of our jobs, or the identity that our social circle has embraced, or some freshly propagated philosophy (none of which we're really paying all that much attention to anyway). We've come to passively assume such prefabricated currents as a trusted norm that we thoughtlessly join, rather than seeing them as a force of factors that we should wisely mitigate. Or we pay no attention to the actual current at all, rather focusing on the things that come along as we move in and with the current itself. Are we paying attention enough to realize that we may not be paying attention?

As this thing called life moves 'round about us, and as we move 'round about within it, are we paying attention to it all? Are we paying attention, or have we unwittingly confused a host of other behaviors and habits as paying attention? Are we paying attention, or have we adopted certain views or biases as ready templates that we slap on life in order to explain it, instead of paying attention in order to understand it? Are we paying attention, or has our cadence been set by the stale monotony of habit or the demands of life that are so intrusive that we can't pay attention because the demands are so consuming? Are we paying attention?

We can certainly 'exist' without paying attention, despite the rather dangerous and somewhat spurious nature of such an existence. We can walk in ignorance as a choice that we embrace out of convenience or hold close due to the fact that we choose not to be bothered with things might upset our tediously constructed applecart. But that does not and cannot wave off the larger question that we too often avoid; can we actually 'live' without paying attention?

Paying Attention to Live Fully

It's my sense that most of us want to move through life and actually 'live' life as we move through it. We want the experience of it. We want to taste it. Savor it. To say that we sat at the table and truly drew in the essence of it all. That we set foot on the path and ascended the peaks despite how rocky they might have been and how precarious they may have become. That the summits have been ours and that we have drawn in the fullness of the vistas revealed from those summits as they fell away to golden horizons in every direction. Yes, we want to say that we 'lived' in a way that makes living grand beyond the scope of words to describe.

Yet, there appears to be a seemingly endless litany of people who look at life once it's blown-by and ask what they've really gotten out of it as it blew by. Too many people look over their shoulders and see a whole lot of life behind them, without a whole lot of anything in their hands to show for everything that's behind them simply because they weren't paying attention. There are table missed, summits never ascended, and vistas gone wanting. They then turn and they peer with longing eyes into the future, and in the peering, they don't see enough life left ahead of them to ever make up for what got by them. As massive and robust as life is, it got by them and they didn't even see it in the passing.

It seems that far too often we don't really pay attention. We think we pay attention. We most certainly believe that we pay attention. We would look in the mirror and tell ourselves that we're quite observant and fairly sharp about it all. We feel that we're astute and keen in discerning life as it's coming at us. We watch a myriad of things unfold and applaud ourselves for figuring out that they were unfolding long before they showed up to unfold. We've come this far, and we quite naturally assume that we must have paid some degree of attention in order to get this far. Most of us feel that we're paying attention.

But are we paying attention, or are we doing other things that mimic paying attention? Have we fooled ourselves into believing that we're paying attention, and will we someday wake up to both the shock and inestimable grief of realizing that we were not?

Things That Mimic Paying Attention

Habit Verses Paying Attention

How often are we simply caught in worn-out patterns of behaviors that have nothing to do with paying attention and everything to do with habit? How often are we simply habitually reactionary, doing in this particular instance what we've done in every other instance that came before it? We think that we're paying attention when what we're doing is paying homage to mindless repetition, slothfully assuming that since this response worked before it will work again. Habit makes the heart comatose because the heart doesn't have to pay attention anymore. It's life on cruise-control.

Habit is a whole lot easier than paying attention. For those of us who prefer ease over advancement, habit will address the problem with a whole lot less energy and significantly less time than paying attention would demand of us. Habit is the soul on autopilot, where we have the richness of life fly right by us without a single inking that something is now fading in the rearview mirror that we never even saw out of the front window. Fundamentally, habit demands nothing of us other than we remember what the habit is so that we can reflexively repeat it. And because it demands so little, it leaves us with little.

Ignoring Verses Paying Attention

How often do we feign that we're paying attention when we're actively ignoring what's going on? There are those times in life when whatever's happening isn't all that savory. Sometimes things aren't all that fun. Sometimes things are a drudgery. Sometimes things will demand something of us that we're tired of giving. And because life does this, whatever's coming at us is something that we'd prefer were moving away from us. There are times when we just don't care to care, and so we turn a blind eye and walk away.

And at these times we pretend that we're paying attention so that we're not looking irresponsible, or lax, or plain stupid. Often, we're not paying attention on purpose. We can look invested, and appear concerned, and present as attentive when we're frankly ignoring the whole distasteful situation. And in ignoring it, what we're doing is hoping that it will rapidly pass into the foggy recesses of our lives and our memories without disturbing our lives in the passing. Ignorance is walking the edge of a cliff on a cloudy night, and instead of ascending we find ourselves rapidly descending.

Assuming Verses Paying Attention

Sometimes we think we're paying attention when what we're doing is assuming. We draw conclusions, or craft opinions, or develop points of view about something. And in doing so, we assume that we could not have drawn these conclusions, or crafted these opinions, or developed these points of view without the information to do so. And so, we assume that the only reason that we have the information is because we've been paying attention.

Yet far too often we're not really paying attention at all. Rather, we're drawing from past experiences, or preconceived biases, or the opinion of some social group that we've aligned ourselves with. We've heard rumors, or read something somewhere, or just have this gut-level feeling about something. It's what this person would say, or what this organization would do, or what this belief system would dictate. And while all of this can have some degree of value, it cannot replace the need to pay attention so that the decisions we make are based on relevant, timely and factual information rather than the muddied slurry of other things.

Following Verses Paying Attention

Finally, often what we're really paying attention to is where everyone else is going. We're paying strict attention to the trends and we heed all things vogue and chic. We're focusing on the colorful declarations of some group, or the rants on Social Media, or the opinions of some celebrity, or the united convictions of some philosophy that we've embraced. We want to know where everyone else is going with whatever this is so that we can escape any real thinking by letting the group decide for us while staying in lockstep with the group so we don't appear too odd.

In these situations, we're certainly paying attention. But we're paying attention to others who probably aren't paying much attention because too often they're focused on biased agendas verses ferreting out pure truth. We've aligned ourselves with an array of sources that have molded some pretty convincing looking truth out of some pretty pathetic agendas. And these people walk tight circles in front of the mountains in front of them, thinking that they're climbing while they're spending the whole of their lives circling. And I don't think we want to pay attention to that.

Start Paying Attention

To live is to observe, despite the risk in what we'll find and in spite of the disappointment that the finding often brings. To experience the fullness of life is to thrust oneself out into the fullness of life. To embrace the wholeness of this journey is to lift your head, squint your eyes, wipe your heart free of bias, pull away the lens of agendas and look. And in the looking we might be profoundly challenged, but if we adhere to truth, we will never be disappointed that we looked. If we stand on the principles of scripture, looking will never be too difficult. Rather, it can be exhilarating.

When you pay attention, you'll never have to worry about looking over your shoulder and seeing a whole lot of life behind you, without a whole lot of anything in your hands to show for everything that's behind you.

You won't miss the tables or the summits. And that will be the case because you took the time to pay attention.

Chapter Six
Life
What's the End Game?

"This is good, and pleases God our Savior, who wants all people to be saved and to come to a knowledge of the truth."
I Timothy 2: 3-4 (NIV)

"The Bible tells us that Jesus Christ came to do three things. He came to have my past forgiven, you get a purpose for living and a home in Heaven."
Rick Warren

It's inevitable. Sooner or later our lives will be over. The day will come when we will reach the last minute of the last day on the last page of the calendar of our lives. Sooner or later we will all have that single day when 'tomorrow' won't be standing at the ready to become the next 'today.' Every single day of our existence has always been marked by the reality of another day to the point that we have assumed a 'forever' inventory of other days. Tomorrow is assumed to be inevitable, which means that we have lost the sense that tomorrow is a gift of the most fragile and precious sort.

Yet, the seemingly bottomless inventory from which we have repeatedly drawn our days will one day be wholly and irretrievably expended, and what we have never faced we will now face. Sooner or later our lives will be over.

Lives Defined by Tasks

At that point, the daily obligations and challenges that both defined and drove our lives will come to an abrupt end. All of the assorted tasks, the innumerable problems, the incessant obstacles, the various celebrations, the breaking and making of relationships, the paying down of mortgages, the paying out of compliments, and all of the things that consumed both our thoughts and our time will be forevermore concluded.

And in the conclusion, what is going to be left other than the conclusion of all of these things that are now concluded? We've checked off the proverbial boxes on the endless pages that now lay as thick reams at our feet. Standing in the pile of papers past, we suddenly find that we've checked off the last box behind which there are no other boxes because there are no other pages. Standing with that final page in hand, we abruptly realize that life will not afford us additional pages to pencil in other boxes that would somehow press the end of our lives out another ream or two. And now the single question becomes, "What's left?"

The Tally of What We Got Done

If all that's left is an endless litany of tasks accomplished and problems overcome, then the tally of our lives is the tally of what we got done. We suddenly find that we had lived out the sum total of our days bowing to the stale tedium of checklists. Life had burgeoned into a banally conditioned existence, mechanically pounding out prescribed tasks that we, or life, or circumstance, or others had penned on the reams that chronicled our life. We completed a bunch of stuff, most of which didn't really matter at the end. Yes, it was impressive. But impressive toward what end? What is the summation of these tasks other than the completion of them? What did they change and what did they leave behind other than stuff that got done?

And all of this we had mistakenly taken as living. Life has now fallen into the dramatically expanding backlog of history that tediously records achievements accomplished and dutifully stores them in the catacombs of history as life now completed. With the reams now chronicled and forever filed away, they are soon lost to the dementia of history and the flood of life now surging on without us. We checked the boxes, but did we live? And we dare not confuse the two.

Life too often becomes parched, rote and stale as if the sum total of the goal is simply getting through life, rather than the far greater goal of irreversibly transforming life as the singular goal of the journey itself. We live to live life, but not change it. We live to figure out its cadence, not transform it. We live to create a comfortable place, rather than dare to discover our place. We live to be good, but not to be great. We live to win, which means that we've forsaken what it is to succeed. We live without a calling because we didn't deem it of enough importance to ask God what it was and how we fulfill it. We checked a bunch of boxes, but we didn't live.

A Calling

Do we live solely to check off the relentless list of incessant obligations that life pens on the pages of our lives? Have we drearily defined life as something more of a strictly linear course where we begin at one point and methodically plod in a single direction in single steps until we reach a single point? And if this cycle is the sum total of our existence, is it simply existence that we errantly took for living? Have we chosen to be that ignorant and therefore squander our lives out of that ignorance? And if it is simply existence, have we completely confused authentically robust living with something more akin to a robotic subsistence?

The demands of life both gently lull and aggressively coerce us into some sort of nauseatingly methodical regime that becomes the cadence to which we live our lives. Mesmerized into some catatonic state by pandemic routine, we lose a vision for anything else other than pandemic routine. In fact, we may see life as being nothing else because we can see nothing more. And in it all an exhilarating sense of calling is lost.

The Core of a Calling

A calling calls us to charge the world rather than solely walk in blind lockstep with it. A calling is a declared rebellion of sorts where we purposefully engage life's routine with the unrelenting intent to wildly transform the routine itself. It is the clarion call to embrace good things in order to make them great things, to believe that wherever we are is not even remotely close to where we could be and should be. A calling declares that a strictly linear course can be majestically swept upward by wonder, breathlessly elevated by vision, and potently energized by faith.

A calling is a brilliant and entirely undimmed vision that breathlessly engages this existence of ours. In the engagement, it staunchly refutes the stale mundaneness of survival, and it outright rejects surrender to the blandness of rote living. It loudly declares that there is infinitely more to all of this and that we have been specifically ordained to boldly usher that 'more' into our own existence. The unashamedly audacious nature of a calling goes far beyond us, tasking us with the far greater obligation of unashamedly infusing that 'more' directly into the existence of others. It is a surrender to the great God of great callings, who has not created a single life without gifting it with a calling in the creating. And in altering our own existence as well as transforming that of others by clothing ourselves in such a calling, we do nothing less than change the whole of our world. That is a calling. That is our calling.

Sooner or later our lives will be over. And rather than a checklist of assorted accomplishments that lays as thick reams at my feet, I would much rather have a tally of how radically different life is because I robustly lived out my calling and changed the world around me. And I achieved that feat by engaging the world out of the raw energy and electric vision generated by a calling that God granted me eons before He birthed me.

Do I Have a Calling?

No one need ask if they have a calling, for all of us have been bequeathed with a calling of grand proportions. We may at times state that we don't have one or that life has somehow bypassed us in the area of a calling. However, such a view is often birthed of fear and fed by trepidation as we know that a calling will demand sacrifice. We typically loathe the idea of embracing the repercussions and pain of sacrifice. So we live in passive denial, living out our lives in a state of perpetual avoidance and forever wallowing in the stale compliance of norms, thereby abandoning the greatness that was ours. Simply put, ignore your calling and you forfeit your life.

The issue is not having a calling. The issue is in boldly setting out to discover it, embracing the whole of if without the fear that its size would impart, and living it out despite the inherent costs that are certain to be ours to endure in accepting it. It is about living above our line of sight. It's about living beyond the reach of our vision. It's about living outside of that which provides us comfort.

And such living will settle for nothing less than the wholesale transformation of the very thing that we've called living. To do anything else is to exist only, and mere existence is nothing more than opportunity forever squandered, and life forfeited. To seize a calling is seize adventure of the greatest sort. It is to leave an enduring legacy that is far beyond lifeless reams of paper detailing now concluded achievements. It is in reality to leave a world transformed because we ourselves dared to be transformed. And it was all because of a calling heeded and a calling obeyed.

Identifying Our Calling

One very effective way to identify your calling is to ask yourself what do you spend your time running from? What have you repeatedly avoided? What have you perpetually ignored? What have you persistently pushed off to another day that never becomes 'the' day? What is it that have you attempted to replace with a dizzying array of things that never replace it?

It's not that we don't understand our calling. In fact, it is our running that evidences the fact that at some level we do understand it. A calling is consuming, demanding, relentless and uncompromising. It will hand you everything you could hope for, but it will demand everything that you hope in. In a world drowning in trinkets marketed as treasure, next to God our calling is the single greatest thing that we could ever hope to engage. And when something so frighteningly magnificent calls, the frailness of our humanity kicks in and we run. Your calling is calling. Are you listening or are you fleeing? Because if you're fleeing, your will live within the box of fear. If you listen, you'll never know what a box is.

Chapter Seven
What I've Learned
Just by Watching

"Jesus sat down opposite the place where the offerings were put and watched the crowd putting their money into the temple treasury. Many rich people threw in large amounts. But a poor widow came and put in two very small copper coins, worth only a few cents. Calling his disciples to him, Jesus said, "Truly I tell you, this poor widow has put more into the treasury than all the others. They all gave out of their wealth; but she, out of her poverty, put in everything—all she had to live on."

- Matthew 12-41-44 (NIV)

"One must always be aware, to notice—even though the cost of noticing is to become responsible."

- Thylias Moss

We are not a terribly observant lot. And we are not because we are focused on speaking into life instead of letting life speak into us. We have our well-oiled agendas, and we have honed our biases to a razors-edge. We know what we want (for the most part), and we've effectively tied those wants to a rather harrowing sense of entitlement. Therefore, it's not that we 'want' those things. Rather, it's that we're owed them (in our minds anyway).

We presume that life is ours for the taking, so we pillage it until we're starved by the very choices that we thought would feed us. We force-fit our tiny rubrics over this immense existence of ours until we've confused the box we've created for the existence we failed to mimic. We think that life is ours to create to our specifications, when it's far more about the privilege that we have to discover what's already been created by God's infinite specifications. Our running list of demands is relentlessly demanding, leaving us on a myopic hunt for what we want instead of finding out what life wants to give us.

We tediously create calendars filled with empty duties, and then we foolishly let those calendars empty us. We're running with no clear place to which we're running, which leaves us running in circles, running in place, and running on empty. We chase whatever grants us the accolades of others so that we might feel good about ourselves. We heed the trends, follow what's vogue, walk in step with whoever's walking around us, and we end our days exhausted realizing that whatever we were seeking was, yet again, not found. No, we are not a terribly observant lot because we're far too occupied with that which is occupying us.

We focus on things that support what we want life to be and how we want to see it all. We judiciously turn a blind-eye and a deaf-ear to anything that questions our plans, confronts our values, or disrupts our cherished agendas. We live careening toward the precipice of certain disaster with cautions lifting themselves all around us. Yet, their messages grate against our precious agendas, so they are not heard and our pending destruction remains fully intact.

We're not a terribly observant lot. Rather, we're a myopic lot. We're settled into our tiny rubrics that feed our view of life and protect that view from something that might challenge it, but something that might likewise raise it. We wish to press everything else into a forever oblivion from which is will never rise and therefore never challenge us. No, we're not a terribly observant lot and our lives will die the death of ignorance and agendas gone astray unless we commit to change.

The Right Priorities to See the Right Things

It's really rather simple. The essential things that we need are not things that we create. Our arrogance gets the better of us and we think that we must create what we need. If we don't, we believe that we are eternally doomed to live out our lives in perpetual peril due to the supposed absence of those things. And to add insult to injury, we believe that somehow, we are endowed with the superior ability to create those things. We live a two-fold deception. First, that we understand our situation enough to know what the solutions are. And two, that we actually have it within our power and our intellect to create those solutions. The fact is, we have neither and will be destroyed by both if we refuse to acknowledge those realities.

We'd be terribly wise to humble ourselves a bit and realize that the fundamental things that we need were already there meeting our needs long before we ever recognized our need of them. They're there. God created an existence comprehensive beyond comprehension. And in that existence, He placed Himself so that we have access to everything in the whole of existence. What we need lays all around us. The ingredients to every problem, the tools for every task, the seeds of whatever needs to be birthed, the salve for everything that needs to be healed. All of that lays all around us. We just have to watch for them and learn from them.

When we don't watch, we don't grow…at least in ways that are healthy. Life naturally abounds with rich lessons, bold ideas, life-altering principles, cautions and warnings, lessons and lectures. Preemptively interwoven into this ingeniously crafted existence is everything that we need to be everything that we are. Indeed, life is the perfect tutorial. We don't have to create anything. All we have to do is watch and learn. But to do that, we have to 'watch'. And that is a skill that most of us need to hone.

What I've Learned by Watching

Recently I wrote a letter to my two children on the eve of their respective birthdays. And as I wrote this letter, what I realized in the writing was that I was simply sharing what I had learned by watching. We won't learn everything, for life is far too vast for that. But we can learn more than enough. In the watching, I discovered that while I haven't learned everything, I've learned what I needed to learn.

Life is not about learning everything. Rather, it's about learning what's essential for 'now'. In life's grandly choreographed dance, what's essential for 'now' will automatically and quite seamlessly build upon what's essential for the future.

And while I've not honed the skill of watching sufficiently, I'm learning it. Not perfectly by any stretch, but enough to glean some precious lessons. If we avoid all of the pitfalls discussed above, and if we commit to watch, we will begin to learn a few things. And in looking around a bit, here's what I've learned:

- At their core people are good. They may not see it and they may not act on it, but there is always great good somewhere within them.

- I must meet people where they are at and not expect them to meet me where I am at. This is the art of relationship.

- Revenge never works. I must rest in the fact that God is the "Just Judge" and that I can leave it to Him to perfectly right every wrong.

- If I let God define success I will truly be successful, for my definitions of success often represent my lack of vision and my disparaging tendency to be selfish.

- Sometimes my successes come quickly and at other times they are terribly slow to arrive. It is not my place to determine the speed at which they arrive or if they arrive at all. My place is to keep forging ahead no matter what.
- Perfection is impossible. Therefore, I do not

strive for perfection. What I strive for is to give one-hundred-percent of myself in everything that I do. If I do that, I have asked everything of myself I can ask.

- If I rise above what people do to me, and consistently strive to be the 'bigger man' despite the cost to me, I will never become what I dislike in others.

- There is always hope, even when I can't see it. And if I act on that truth, there is no obstacle or challenge that has the power to defeat me.

- If I put others first, I will never find myself being last.

- Life is not random, as there is a phenomenal plan for my life that was laid out before the beginning of time. And if I seek it out and then live it out, I will live the most powerful and robust life imaginable.

Embrace What Life Shows You

Finally, when you watch, accept that what you see is in fact what you need. There will be times when life will teach us what we'd prefer not to learn. It will take us on routes previously unknown to us. It will demand the best of us knowing that comfort will bring out the worst in us. It will say 'yes' to places where a frightened world says 'no', and it will say 'no' to places where a selfish world says 'yes'. It will counter your beliefs at times and buoy them at others. It will press you to precipices that you have spent your life avoiding, and it will show you precipices that you had no idea were there. It will grow you in ways that you have long resisted, and at other times it will grow you in ways that you've sought to grow all of your life.

But to learn both that which is comforting and that which is not is to meticulously round us out as people in ways that few are rounded out. Let life set the agenda, write the curriculum and be the teacher, for it has both precious and phenomenal lessons standing ready for you. You simply need to watch. So…start watching.

Chapter Eight
Here's Where I Stand
To Be Bold

"Have I not commanded you? Be strong and courageous. Do not be afraid; do not be discouraged, for the LORD your God will be with you wherever you go."

- Joshua 1:9 (NIV)

"Avoiding danger is no safer in the long run than outright exposure. The fearful are caught as often as the bold."

- Helen Keller

It seems that the idea of taking a stand is perpetually taking a beating. The whole idea of taking a stand is driven by the conviction that at certain times the need to take a stand is unarguably undeniable and inescapably inescapable. Taking a stand is taking a risk, and sometimes a big one. It's the proverbial "stepping out on a limb" when we'd prefer not to climb the tree in the first place. It's "facing the fire" when we've lived out the entirety of our lives being told not to play with matches. It's being told to "step up to the plate" when the only plates that we have any interest in stepping up to are the ones with food on them. Therefore, too often instead of taking a stand we try to take the shortest route directly out of wherever we've found ourselves standing.

On the other side of that dilemma, we know full well that if we don't take a stand at those inescapable moments, and if we hightail it out of there, there's no other way to define our lack of action other than that of gross cowardice. Limbs, fires, or plates...it's all the same. Each requires that we move to some place of discomfort in order to face something uncomfortable. And we're rather adverse to that because the label of cowardice sticks for a long, long time. Nonetheless, not many people take a stand.

Calculating the Risk, Verses Living Out the Conviction

We seem to be a bit hesitant to center ourselves too firmly on one issue, or on some conviction, or on a belief system of some sort. It seems that we much prefer to loosely position ourselves so that we can sway in unison with the opinions and convictions of others. We like to leave ample to room to 'bob and weave' just in case our stance becomes a little too offensive or potentially alienating to those around us. We can readily disappear if things get too hot.

Yes, we want to take a stand, but we also want to be able to stay in the good graces of everyone who's watching us do it. We want to take a stand, but in doing so we don't want to look too antiquated, or too outlandish, or too different, or too controversial, or too anything that might estrange us from everyone else. There's an endearing degree of camaraderie that we want to maintain with the rest of the humanity. We might rub someone the wrong way, but we don't want to rub too hard (if we have to rub at all). Too often, the need to exercise caution so that we don't place ourselves too far outside of everyone else's good graces overrides our core convictions. We opt to be seen as 'right' in the eyes of everyone else, rather than doing what's 'right' in light of the situation. No, not many people take a stand.

Calculated Stands are Fake Stands

Sure, we take stands. But we take calculated stands. We take safe stands. We take stands that certainly look like stands, and we play the boldly rogue and rather chivalrous part of someone who's taking a stand, but we take stands that are reasonably palatable to those around us. We want to be praised for taking a stand, but we don't want to be persecuted for taking a stand. We want to be admired, but we don't want to be attacked. We want to be seen as gallant and terribly brave, but we don't want to be viewed as stupid and wildly ignorant. We want to take a stand that costs us nothing. We want to play the part, but we want to avoid paying for the part. However, nothing of this sort is ever a stand.

Or we want to take stands to covertly elevate ourselves rather than elevate the cause that we claim to stand for. The entirety of the cause becomes 'us,' (whatever 'us' happens to be). The actual cause is what we will gain in fighting for the cause that we purport to support. Therefore, the original cause becomes nothing more than a vehicle that we've hijacked to elevate our agenda. And in such an egotistical move, we would be wise to remember that if we are the sum total of the cause that we claim to embrace, we have chosen the least of all things to stand for. The cause of 'self' at the expense of all else will always be far too small to squander our lives in the pursuit of, and it will never be worth the sacrifice that it will ultimately demand.

Despite the fraudulent nature of these kinds of stands, we nonetheless want to be able to raise high the standard and decisively plant our flags firmly in the ground and boldly declare that this is the hill that we're willing to die on. We want to raise our heads high, fix our feet firmly, and adamantly refuse to retreat a single inch from this hard-won ground. And the desire to have such a glorious victory is so engrained in so many of us that we are pressed to circumvent the fear of rejection by embracing the lie of fraudulence. We think that we're raising the standard on some bloodied hilltop when the fact of the matter is that we're doing neither. No, not many people take a stand.

A Calculated Stand is Not a Stand

A calculated stand is not a stand, nor can it be (despite how much we might wish it to be). It is never close to anything even remotely resembling an authentic stand. Living for a calculated stand is living with the illusion that we're living. It's scripting something, rather than being a part of something so big that we could never hope to script it. We can't script ethics. We can't write out prescriptions for that which God imprinted across the whole of creation at its inception. It's leagues beyond our ability to create something that's expansive enough to grant us a lifetime of running room. A calculated stand is not a stand.

A stand means that we have a belief that's so deep and so core to the entirety of our existence that the most infinitesimal compromise entirely and completely guts the belief. It means that we've got a conviction that is so thoroughly rooted in the very foundation of our existence that it simply can't be shaken by the culture regardless of how hard the culture shakes it. Taking a stand means that we've determined our values to be infinitely more precious and incalculably more valuable than any price we might even come close to paying in any kind of stand that we can take on their behalf. Taking a stand means that we hold to something and believe in something to the point that any cost that we might incur in standing for this thing will pale in comparison to the thing that we're standing for. Taking a stand means that not taking a stand simply cannot stand. That's what it means to take a stand, and sadly not many people take a stand.

Taking a Stand is Standing Against Something

Taking a stand means that we're standing against something, but conversely it means that something is standing against that which we are standing for. This can create a violently adversarial dynamic, and typically we're not all too fond of adversity. Yet, what makes a stand a stand in the truest sense of the word is that that which I'm standing for cannot occupy the same ground as that which I'm standing against. Therefore, if I chose not to stand, the very thing that I'm standing for risks being eliminated because of my cowardice and wiped out because of my selfish concerns. No, not many people take a stand.

What Do I Want to Stand For?

Taking a Stand

First, I want to stand for taking a stand. I want to believe that we are not just passive people floating through life on the sordid winds of culture and trends and all things vogue and comfortable. I want to stand on the belief that we can be game changers when the game is changing long-standing values and long-sustaining beliefs. I want to stand on the conviction that our convictions can drive us in and through whatever gale-force headwind the culture has unleashed against us. I stand for the fact that we can take a stand, and in the standing we become the embodiment of the very principles that we stand for.

One Human Being Taking a Stand is More Powerful than a Thousand Who Are Not

I want to stand for the belief that a single human being taking a stand possesses a collective power greater than a thousand people who don't. I stand for the belief that the world is altered, entire cultures are shifted, history is realigned, and innumerable lives are transformed as a result of the power that is unleashed when a single person takes a stand. A single person taking a stand proclaims a value or a conviction in a language that completely eclipses any language known to man. A solitary person taking a stand for all things true and right embodies a bravery that lends a potent credibility and an unassailable validity to whatever it is that they're standing for. And if we stand long enough and hard enough, it inspires those around us to thirst with an unquenchable thirst for that kind of conviction as well.

Ethics and Morals Stand Above all Else Even When They Stand Alone

I want to stand for the fact that absolute truths and core values stand even when everything else in all of existence leaves them standing utterly alone. I stand for the truth that too often the majority stands for that which is easy and convenient and globally acceptable, and that quite often it is the few who refuse to surrender to such superficial and toxic notions. I stand on the conviction that compromise is the root of great things, and that attempting to negotiate timeless values is the product of thoughtless arrogance. I want to stand on the foundation of ethics and morals when the world around me would assault that foundation with all of its collective might, and in the standing I want to stand on the truth that that foundation will stand long after everything that has assailed it has itself has ceased to stand.

God Has Designed Us to Stand

Most importantly, I want to stand on the truth that God has designed us to stand, and that the opportunity to stand is the opportunity to live exuberantly and gloriously. That our very natures are hewn and shaped and honed to be raised up when everything around us is falling down. I want to stand on the belief that great things are the product of ordinary people who are made great when they stand. I want to stand because God designed me to stand, and I want to stand in and on His design. I want to stand because doing anything else is standing down. May we all stand and may we all recognize that when we stand together nothing can stand against us.

Chapter Nine
The Battle
Choosing Wisely

"He trains my hands for battle; my arms can bend a bow of bronze."
- Psalm 18:34

"Some of the greatest battles will be fought within the silent chambers of your own soul."
- Ezra Taft Benson

The Battles Without

Battles come every day. In whatever form they come, they come. They come with relentless pressure, incessantly assailing the battlements of our lives and our culture. Battles come in our marriages, in our families, in our jobs, in our communities and in our friendships. Enemies violently storm our lives, startlingly surging out of places and people and situations that we never dreamt they would surge from. Dark storm clouds gather over the horizon of politics, and enemies marshal their forces and assail our economy. Deteriorating ethics and collapsing morals perpetually weaken walls that have long protected the integrity of our culture, permitting enemies of all sorts frightening entrance in places we once assumed as invincible. When one battle appears to be ebbing in one place, another always seems to be brewing in another.

The Battles Within

Then there are the battles around our own thoughts. We're constantly pressing against the desire to feed that voraciously hungry dark side of ourselves and perpetrate a great wrong in order to feed it. It seems that we are incessantly faced with vexing questions and draining decisions that seem to be intentionally designed to batter the bulwark of our morals at every turn. We are constantly faced with choices that stretch our ethics to the breaking point, effortlessly snapping the very back of those ethics as we succumb to our baser self and then grapple with the guilt that suffocates us once we've caved.

Battles Within Battles

There are battles within battles that become horribly tangled and impossibly enmeshed, radically elevating the complexity of situations to near insanity and beyond. We are confronted with battles that are less battles and more points of irritation, all too frequently being the result of sloppy living on our part or on the part of someone else. There are battles fought for the sole purpose of staging the next battle or provoking one. Battles rage for the purpose of strategically positioning a person, or a philosophy, or a cause, thereby rendering victory little more than a secondary objective. Often battles are fought for the singular purpose of forcing cherished societal issues to the forefront, repositioning political opponents, solidifying allies, courting world favor, or simply to make a statement. Indeed, battles abound.

Giving Battles Permission

Far too often these enemies seize perpetually higher ground right in middle of innumerable masses of people who ignore both the savagery of the battle, as well as the horrific consequences of the very battle that rages all around them. Too often it's not that we lose battles, or fight them ineptly, or flee in panicked fashion away from them. Rather, as impossible and improbable as it sounds, it's often the case that we ignore their very existence despite the screaming ferocity of them. In reality, the greatest tragedy may not be the battle itself and the carnage that it wreaks. Rather, the far greater tragedy may be our intentional ignorance of the battle. It would seem that a weak defense is hardly the worst-case scenario. Not recognizing the battle in the first place is clearly the most dangerous scenario of all.

The Enemy as Providential Progression

The increasingly frightening nature of the battle's rests not simply in the abject ignorance of many as to the battle itself, but it rests with those who write off the battle as the natural progression of the culture to some higher consciousness and more refined state of democracy. There are those who view the onset of destructive forces as possessing the essential elements and irresistible energy that has both the method and muscle to perpetuate the evolutionary process that is certain to birth a more robust and advanced society. And in viewing these battles in this manner the battle is dismissed and the need to step up and fight it need not be considered.

We tend to embrace this view in our own personal growth as well, viewing progressive thinking as the force that will breach the barriers to our own maturation. We somehow sense that it is in the abandonment of something that we open the door to something better. That the idea of 'new' immediately places previously held beliefs in the category of 'old.' That progression hinges on applying these definitions to things that are, in fact, timeless and therefore rendering them as 'out-of-time.' We quickly forget that our definition of time is irrelevant regarding things that are timeless, and that the application of such irresponsible definitions at the cost of that which we are defining is certain to be our undoing.

However, it is the opinion of some that it is in the tearing down that the building up most effectively occurs. Indeed, such a belief certainly has great validity if the tearing down rests in the hands of a morality that realizes that immorality can most certainly tear down, but it does not have within itself the character to rebuild. Therefore, what is destructive is errantly seen as good in that whatever might be destructive about it is offset by the good that our agenda purports it will bring. Such skewed nonsense embraces the enemy as importing a hidden good that offsets the destructive nature of the enemy.

Morals as Restraining

There appears to be some deliriously cock-eyed sense that true advances are only restrained by the values that birthed them, so to battle on behalf of them is to battle against progress itself. Too often, 'out with the old and in with the new' embraces a supposed vision that is far too often void of the wisdom that is critically necessary to determine if indeed it is a vision at all. Or rather, in reality is it little more than a hollow idea borne of selfishness, tainted by all thing's vogue, and erected on the teetering foundation of bias. We may gorge ourselves on philosophies that bend truth to serve bent agendas and that give us permission to side-step core values, making our enemy a friend that we accidently mistook as an enemy. When this happens foe becomes friend, and the soft underbelly of all that we stand for becomes dangerously exposed.

Letting Battles Be Battles

The most egregious thing that we can do is to reinterpret a battle that we should fight as some glorious advancement that we need to get behind, instead of seeing it as something that we need to get behind us. I would conjecture that the greatest cowardice is to cow-down in the face of the battles that are facing us and to set about changing the face of them so that the battle becomes invisible. In doing so, we can therefore live without the guilt of having run away. If we choose to succumb through surrender borne of reconstructed thinking, or should we rationalize unadulterated defection by shifting our values and pitching compromise, we will live diminished lives scarred by defeat and undercut by failure. And in the end, the victories that we were bred to win will become defeats that we will be doomed to bear.

We need to let battles be battles and refuse to let them be anything else. We need to view battles through the keen eyes of morals and the honed intuition of ethics, rather than viewing battles with an eye toward changing those very morals and values. We must not allow ourselves to become deluded into believing that core morals and sound values are irreparably bound to another time that would bind all forward thinking and decisively banish forward progression. We cannot be duped by the evasive arguments that rationalize the abandonment of cherished morals and ethics because they will serve to turn the clock backward rather than creating a potent framework to thrust us forward.

The Truth of Morals and Values

In order to do that, we must boldly recognize that morals and values do not impede progress or stall advancement. Standing on solid principles as we stand on the precipice of the future is not a clarion call wherein we are compelled to retreat to the comfort of more secure or simpler times. Instead, morals and values create the potently sustaining bulwark within which our future can be securely and successfully navigated. Any future stripped of morals and purged of values is a future that will become an abhorrent past that will lend shame to our stories and paint regret across the face of history.

A Word of Caution

And it will be so because the greater our advances, the more necessary the cultivation of morals and values to shape them and guide those advances. The further we advance the more vulnerable we become due to the simple fact that we possess progressively greater power that brings progressively greater implications in both the use and abuse of that power. Therefore, the further we progress the greater the need for the sure and faithful guidance of morals and ethics.

We cannot permit any argument despite how astutely conceived and tediously constructed to cause us to see enemy as friend. We must understand that it is the power of ethics embraced and morals unleashed that transform individual lives and unleash entire cultures toward rich transformation. Let the enemy be the enemy and let us stand in opposition as we are called to do so. Let us never live in denial of the battles that rage around us and within us. Indeed, let's allow the battle to be the battle and in doing so, let us boldly engage it.

Chapter Ten
The Battle
I'd Rather Be David

"David said to the Philistine, 'You come against me with sword and spear and javelin, but I come against you in the name of the LORD Almighty, the God of the armies of Israel, whom you have defied."

- I Samuel 17:45

"You have to face a giant to become one."

- Johnnie Dent Jr.

Battles are both the bane and the glory of our existence. We adamantly abhor them when they're forced on us by vengeful adversaries who mean us all the harm they can muster up, or when they randomly befall us through indiscriminately cruel circumstances over which we have no control. On the other hand, we rather bask in them when there's something gallantly heroic about them, or they serve to right a great wrong. Sometimes they prove our strength. At other times they expose our weaknesses. Indeed, battles are both the bane and glory of our existence.

Battles as Daily Challenges

The battles that we fight come in all shapes and sizes. Some are nothing more than things we would define as the day in and day out challenges of living out our lives. We've come to see these battles as a natural and acceptable element of life and living. It's finding the right job, or working out the knotty kinks in a relationship, or tediously molding the mind of an entrenched teen, or wrestling with entirely opposing choices that will ultimately leave us with a loss no matter which choice we make. Although these kinds of battles can be acutely troubling and unduly painful, they become something less than battles and something more akin to the ordinary ebb and flow of life that swirls around each of us in either gentle rivulets or turbulent undertows.

Battles as Battles

But then there are those things that have little or nothing to do with the natural course of life and living. There are these acutely harrowing moments either forged on the anvil of our poor choices, or violently struck on the revengeful anvil of someone or something else. There are those things borne of us or borne far outside of us that force us into a maelstrom that we don't have the speed or ingenuity to outrun. These are those events that are not about pressing through to the next thing, rather they are about surviving so that we can get to the next thing. These are those moments when the whole notion of progression is completely swallowed up in the far greater crisis of unadulterated survival.

Battles of Justice

Then there are also those battles that we choose to engage in. It may well be that nothing has advanced against us, or challenged us, or stands looming over us armed to the teeth with crushing intent. The cause of the current battle may have nothing to do with an external force as it may be prompted by an entirely internal one. It may be that we have witnessed a searing injustice, or that a line has been crossed that should never have been crossed. It may arise from something strong bullying something weak and thereby creating a litany of traumatized victims strewn along the road that we likewise trod. It may be the recognition of some destructive force running unchallenged and we feel called to step out, step in its way, and hopefully step on it. Any number of these things enflame our ire and prompt us to step into the fray.

Battles of Calling

Or we may sense some innate calling that's compelling beyond any of our best efforts to resist. There might be a compulsion borne of some deep inner essence that whispers that this battle is the culmination of our very existence; or that this battle represents the essence of the battles for which we've been called, and which are yet to come. We sense that we were "born for such a time as this" (Esther 4:14, NIV) and for battles such as this regardless of the time in which they come. Such a belief empowers us beyond that which we could have imagined. It may well be that engulfing conviction that calls us to right a wrong that has been granted slothful permission to keep breathing, or to wage a single war in order to stop a hundred others that would otherwise follow. Of warrior stock or not, we may feel an irresistible call to a battle either large or small.

The Goliath's Superiority

Whatever the nature of the battle or the circumstances that set the various forces careening against each other, sooner or later we will all fight a battle. And it seems that in fighting these battles of ours, we've developed a mentality of superior warfare. There's something in our construct that envisions what superiority is, whether that's sheer numbers, or the extent of our resources, or timing, or any of an innumerable number of things. It seems that we tend to judge the value of the battle, the potential sacrifice in the battle, and the likely outcome based on how we've defined superiority. This is more akin to a Goliath mentality.

Clearly, wisdom would dictate inventorying such resources as held up against whatever foe we face. Yet, I would wonder if this idea of superiority elevates itself above our convictions, our calling, our sense of justice, and the whole notion that we were raised up to lay ourselves down. Could it be that the calculations that we've devised to determine what battles we will fight or not fight have entirely removed our convictions, our calling, our sense of justice, and the conviction that sacrifice is the pinnacle of any calling? It is possible that we've granted fear a place at the table and elevated personal safety in a manner that battles have become shrewd calculations rather than passionate crusades?

And if that is so, is it possible that we've gutted the very heart the battle? Could it be that any resources that we have will always be secondary to the heart that we have to use those resources? Would it be reasonable to conjecture that any instrument of war, regardless of how devastating, only takes on life when those who hold those weapons are driven by deeply core convictions that bring them to the battlefield? Have we taken passion and conviction and calling (which are the most potent resources of war) off the battlefield? And if we are not driven by those things, is the battle really a battle or is it just a slugfest?

The David's
Battles of Conviction

In that sense, I would much prefer to be David. I would prefer to know my weapon well and be practiced in its use. Yet, I would want the heart behind the weapon so that the nature of the enemy and the weapons arrayed against me do not hold the power for me that they might otherwise hold. I certainly don't want to be foolish or naïve and thoughtlessly take on an enemy without careful consideration of the assets that my enemy possesses. However, I don't want to winch in fear when I need not be fearful. Neither do I want to call a battle lost that is winnable when the core convictions that undergird the weapons that I possess are sufficient to overcome when others would think that I could not and cannot. I much prefer to be David.

It would seem that the greatest victories and the glories that have stood the test of time came on the heels of battles fought of great conviction and deep passion. These are the battle from which stories are spun and heroes arise. It is the common man energized with uncommon conviction that has stood against superior enemies and brought the battle home. And it is not that men weren't wounded and that many perished. It's not that cost wasn't high, for conviction comes with a cost. It's that they won when the world said that they shouldn't have. They won when (from a human perspective) the battlefield was arrayed against them. It's the singularly compelling fact that conviction prevailed over might and stunned those who knew nothing of conviction. I would much prefer to be David.

Admirable Convictions

Yet, many people purport convictions that appear rather dubious and often outright destructive. It would seem that admirable convictions are driven by a greater good, a willingness to lift up another at great cost to self, and to adamantly refuse to dress evil in the garb of good in order to justify one's actions. It may be that in a world of convictions centered on the good of oneself, the gorging of one's own appetite, the spinning of belief systems to serve personal agendas, and the shrewd pabulum spun from these that such agendas have been misinterpreted and embraced as convictions. And when these kinds of convictions are brought to the weapons of war, we are no longer David's.

Our Battles

It may be wise to survey the landscape of our lives, as well as the far greater landscape of the lives around us and ask whether we've fought battles or run from them. And whether our choice has been to fight or flee, where were our convictions and what role did they play or not play in those decisions? And will we bring the lessons from these battles to the one's for which we were crafted to fight, and that loom on the horizons of our lives and our culture? For a life that has forsaken conviction is a life lived in hiding, deaf to purpose, and robbed of victory. It is a life for which a world begging for someone to stand in the gap leaves the gap forever empty. Can I live with myself should I make such choices as these? And the answer is, "I cannot." And since that is the case, I would much prefer to be David.

Chapter Eleven
Abandonment
When People Make Destructive Choices

"He was despised and forsaken of men, a man of sorrows and acquainted with grief; and like one from whom men hide their face He was despised, and we did not esteem Him."

- Isaiah 53:3

"Being abandoned or given up is the most devastating emotion we can cause in another human being."

- Gary David Currie

The Failure of Logic and Reason

There are times when we the best of our logic fails to understand the worst of other's behaviors. It's part of the oddity or maybe complexity of the human psyche that we sometimes make choices that defy any shred of reason or seem void of even the slightest hint of sensibility. More times than we can count we stand in awe of the choices that some people make, standing at some distance shaking our heads in disoriented disbelief and wondering what in the world they were thinking. There are times when we disagree with the actions of others as we would have made a different choice. But then there are other times when the actions of others rise above mere disagreement to utter astonishment as the apparent insanity of their choice's eclipses something as simple as a mere disagreement.

Sometimes our own choices are perplexingly confusing, defying our own logic and leaving us patently bewildered and entirely befuddled at who we are and what we just did. We stand wondering if we stepped aside into something entire alien to us, made a decision in that place, and then came back only to wonder what we just did. Or we look at our decisions in the rearview mirror and we come to understand that the future that we are now in had no bearing on the decision we previously made. Clearly, we can be our greatest puzzle and most mysterious mystery.

At the Expense of Others

Yet, the most inexplicably confounding situations are those when these rather irrational decisions are made at the expense of others. Sure, we can make wildly poor choices that effect ourselves in ways slight or significant. I suppose it's within our rights to chart spurious courses that descend to dark places as long as the only person that ends up in those dark places with us is 'us.' It would seem that we can "shoot ourselves in the foot" as long as it's our foot and no one else's. Yet far too frequently we shoot a lot of other feet other than our own.

And so, the pressing and rather incendiary question becomes, why would we take someone else down with us? What in the world behooves us to make choices that reach out with arms either long or short, grab someone else in whatever way we do that and drag them down? Why do we create a litany of innocent victims whose place of proximity was close enough for us to grab them, wound them as part of whatever our rampage was, and leave them reeling in the emotional carnage that we left them in? Is there some sort of machoistic and sadist alchemy that combines as a means of destroying others in the process of destroying ourselves at the self-same time? Or do we somehow believe that hurting others somehow creates a shared suffering that minimizes our pain by inflicting some of that pain on others, or does it maximize the satisfaction regarding the pain that we're experiencing by knowing that it's duplicated in the life of another?

Why is it that we just can't leave others alone? To the contrary, we find ourselves incessantly goaded by some potent force that's sufficiently compelling to override any sense of responsibility and silence any voice of morality to the point that we pull others in and push them down with issues that aren't even theirs. What compels us to make choices that are certain to seize the course of the life of another and set their path on some dizzying descent?

Self-Preservation

When life presses us with an unnerving intensity, we are reflexively prone to revert to defensive position of self-preservation. Sure, it's quite easy to be graciously gracious and heroically selfless when the cost of doing so isn't all that significant. We can look quite the part when we don't have a lot of skin in the game or when we know that we're not likely to be skinned while we're in the game. We live within limits that are long on self and short on others, so it doesn't take long before we take the shortest route to the closest place of safety. If we ruthlessly strip away all the pleasantries and pretenses that we gaudily wrap ourselves in we will find that self-preservation lays seated underneath it all as the irreparably non-negotiable objective that is so core to the base side of ourselves that we will instinctively sacrifice others to insure it.

Therefore, as the cost/benefit analysis swings away from us, we're more likely to gradually or not so gradually swing the cost over onto others. We're noble, but noble to a point. We're generous, but only to the degree that what we're getting sufficiently offsets what we're giving. We will extend ourselves in ways that appear magnanimous and philanthropic as long as we don't have to extend ourselves beyond arm's reach of ourselves. And these points where we pull up and stop are most often based on our limited tolerance for sacrifice and the degree to which we're willing to absorb pain. There comes a point where the responsibility of accountability is just a bit too revealing, where the selflessness of putting ourselves aside is pinching our egos a bit too hard, and where the concept of sacrifice and the 'good of our fellowman' hasn't given us all that much in return, if it's given us anything at all.

Our Expectations

When the world around us doesn't reciprocate our simple acts of simply being a 'good person' in the manner in which we feel it should, we begin to become toxically jaded and we take a darker turn into ourselves. When the world is perceived by us as intrinsically greedy, when it seems that every action is driven by a darkly covert agenda, and when the rampant selfishness appears wholly unrepentant and entirely irreparable, we pull inward and we put up impenetrable walls. And in putting up the walls we would be quite wise to ask if the things that we find so aberrant and awful are indeed the very things we ourselves engage in. It may well be that our own greed is worse than those that we condemn because we too often demand that we dictate what we give to those around us, we demand how they will (or should) respond to what we have given them, all the while condemning the world of the very offenses that we ourselves are equally guilty of.

If we are not aware of such caustic distortions, we will make it about us. And in making it about us we're foolishly led to believe that all of our many cherished expenditures are never expended because they never move outside of us. It's all about us investing all of 'us' back into all of 'us.' This self-sabotaging, self-absorbing cycle creates an ever-hardening pattern where the deepening pain that we are inflicting on others and the manner in which we are blithely diminishing their lives begins to go entirely unnoticed. Others just don't matter.

Often, we are on the receiving end of such behaviors, and sometimes we're the ones dishing them out. We'd be keenly wise to recognize it in others so that we can more prudently deal with the behaviors as we cope with the impact of them. But we'd be ever wiser to recognize such behaviors in ourselves.

We Are Too Expensive

When we make it about us, someone, somewhere is going to go down simply because the cost of being about 'us' is a cost that will always extend itself beyond 'us.' Someone else is going to pay that. We don't have the life currency to make it about us, so we borrow or steal that 'currency' from other places and other people. Despite our frequently supercilious arguments to the contrary, we simply do not have the inherent capacity to generate everything that we need. However astounding we might perceive it to be, our capacity to independently generate resources will perpetually fall short of the resources that we actually need. Therefore, as our accumulated needs swiftly exhaust our scant resources, we are forced by our limitations to reach outside of ourselves to obtain those resources. And in either borrowing or stealing those resources from someone else, that 'someone' is going down as we attempt to push ourselves up. They pay, and they pay dearly. Or should the tables be turned, we pay in like manner.

Need We Dare Remember

We've regularly failed to realize that being a good person pays exceedingly generous dividends far beyond anything we can borrow or steal. Riches born of sacrifice fill the coffers of heaven. Yet we miss those dividends because they're not exactly the ones that we're looking for, or they've come at some cost when we'd much prefer to receive them free of charge. Often the riches generated are held until time or attitude would render the delivery of them as far more meaningful for us. However, delayed gratification feels much the same as no gratification. And so, cynicism wins the day, pessimism reigns, we become jaded around the edges, and we're going to take others down with us with or without recognizing that we're doing so.

It's quite sad enough that we do things to take ourselves down and shoot ourselves in the foot. Yet, it's infinitely more tragic that we do that to others. We cannot control the actions of others as they perpetrate such behaviors upon us. Yet, we can control ourselves. So, to avoid taking others down we'd be wise to look at the state of our heart, take the temperature of our attitude, and see if our soul is still breathing because we may find that they are all in some state that we'd much prefer them not to be. And once we've inventories them alive again, maybe we'll realize that to sacrifice is to fill the coffers of heaven which will spill over into the vault of our soul. When that happens, we have no need to push others down our wound them because we, by virtue of our sacrifices, have pushed ourselves up without stepping on anyone in order to do it.

Chapter Twelve
Kicking the Can
Ignorance, Denial and Stupidity

"If we are faithless, He remains faithful, for He cannot deny Himself."

- 2 Timothy 2:3 (NIV)

"Now what state do you live in?'

'Denial."

- Bill Watterson, The Essential Calvin and Hobbes: A Calvin and Hobbes Treasury

Face it, there are just some things that we don't like to do. We all have those irritating things that incessantly demand our attention. Every one of us has a collection of loathsome demands that keep throwing themselves in front of us. Our lives are chock full of repetitive tasks, missed agenda items, overdue obligations, lapsed deadlines, and overlooked commitments that constantly harass us. We have a myriad of things that we've repeatedly placed behind us that keep showing up in front of us.

We all have those irritating things that are irritating because we know that they need to be done, and we know that we should have gotten them done a long time ago, and we know that we'd feel a whole lot better if we had gotten them done. But we don't want to. We just don't want to. And so, all of these various things have become something of a noxious stench emanating from the pages of our calendars. Therefore, we find ourselves attempting to pencil those things out and off of our calendars. We want to figure out how we can 'figure them out' of our lives. Where's the place where we can we park these things, walk away from them freed of any and all obligation to them, and know that they're certain to vanish with time? Or conversely, where's the place that we can go to that is so well hidden and stealthy that these things will never be able to find us? We all have things that we just don't like to do, so we kick the can down the road.

There are the messes that we've made. There are the colossal blunders, the erroneous missteps, and the self-centered choices that have turned on us. Then there's the little messes that have grown into mammoth messes because we never took care of the little messes when we should have. There were gambles that we took that were prompted more by a narcissistic headiness than a thoughtful deliberation. There were risks that we embraced out of some childish cavalier notion rather than a measured wisdom. We have some bad things that we caused that we just don't like to deal with, so we want to dispense with them as well. Therefore, we kick all of this down the road as well. Subsequently, the road of our lives becomes congested with more cans than we can ever possibly kick.

Versions of Kicking the Can

Yet, to our chagrin, things don't go away just because we want them to. Problems don't get solved just because we're annoyed with them. Life is not so enchanted that things simply dissipate all by themselves, or mystically resolve themselves because life feels bad for us. Life doesn't have the convenient memory lapses that we often pretend it does, for that would break the bonds of our mistakes and free us up to live as if what happened never happened at all. The idea of the magical eraser that sweeps the whiteboard of our lives clean is nothing more than the manifestation of our escapist mentality unleashed, and the power of our fear running wild.

'Avoidance' is not some sort of practiced slight-of-hand where the things that we're avoiding magically vanish under the silken cloak of avoidance. 'Denial' is not some ingenious, multi-purpose tool that fixes whatever problem is that we're in denial of, somehow busily working away behind the scenes while we're sitting in denial of the problem. And whatever 'ignoring' is, it's not powerful enough to somehow relegate the thing that we're ignoring to the very oblivion that we hope our ignoring will relegate it to. We all have things that we just don't like to do, so we kick the can down the road.

In some sort of ascending insanity, we create more cans as a direct by-product of the denial of the cans that we already have. The road of our lives and our culture is choked with cans that would never have been there had we had the foresight and depth of character to take care of the first cans that showed up. And the fact of the matter is, we can't afford to kick a single can, much less an army of them.

Kicking the Can Implies Acceptance of the Can

In kicking the can, it's not that we're in denial of the issue, or the commitment, or the obligation, or the deadline that we're working so hard to avoid, or the self-made mess that we want to forget about. We've come to accept whatever it is that we're kicking down the road, and we've embraced the fact that it's a part of our lives and it's likely here to stay as much as we hate that. We've long given up hope that it's going to go away, or supernaturally fix itself, or be fixed by someone else.

Kicking the can down the road implies that we're accepted the galling reality that whatever it is that we've avoiding, it's something that's not going to go away; at least on its own. So given that it's not going to go away, we decide to push it away by kicking it down the road. We press it into our future in order to postpone it in our present. However, the illusion rests in the sense that we achieved both, when in fact we accomplished neither.

Kicking the Can Is an Action Based on a Decision

Kicking the can down the road is an action. It represents the decision that we've made about whatever it is that we're avoiding. It's the choice we've made to deal with this thing by not dealing with it. It's a conscious decision to placate responsibility, postpone the inevitable, deny our poor choices, pay a legitimate obligation forward yet again, and momentarily pretend that all is good so as to avoid any discomfort around that fact that all is not good.

There's nothing inherently good or redeeming about kicking the can down the road. In doing so, we're doing nothing more than exhibiting cowardice and nothing less than throwing off responsibility. We're living in some sort of self-imposed denial regarding the need of the can as it sits in the moment. We likewise deny the reality that kicking it into the future doesn't change the need of the moment. Rather, it only encumbers the future at the expense of the moment and the future.

Kicking the Can to Pawn It Off

Sometimes kicking the can down the road is done out of some pathetic hope that somebody else is going to pick it up and take care of it for us. Maybe someone else will step in or step up and solve this. Maybe if we kick it down the road long enough and hard enough somebody else is going to get tired of watching us do it or feel bad enough for us that they'll take care of it. Maybe we're actually kicking the can in the direction of somebody as a means of baiting them a bit and hoping they'll get rid of this for us. Whatever the case, maybe someone will have mercy on us, walk up to the can, pick it up, and dispense of it for us.

We refuse to understand that cans can only be kicked by those who created them. Others can support our denial of the problem, or rationalize our attempts to postpone dealing with them, or somehow legitimize our actions to sooth our conscious. But we can't punt these cans off to anyone because they can't kick them anyway. And maybe part of the most insidious denial is in believing that they can.

Kicking the Can is Often Blaming the Can on Someone Else

Sometimes kicking the can is designed to kick it so far away from us that we no longer look like we're connected to the can. If we can ignore the issue long enough and distance ourselves from it far enough, we can often make it look like we really have nothing to do with it at all. But more than that, it's often a way to distance the issue or the mistake or the blunder so far from us that it actually looks as if it belongs to someone else. Maybe we can ignore the issue long enough and kick it so far away from us that it appears as if it's closer to somebody else than it is to us. If we can place these cans in the proximity of someone else, we can actually associate them with it simply due to their proximity.

If we can pull that off, we can actually make the issue look like it belongs to the person that we've kicked it over to. Sooner or later, we begin to figure out that the longer that we can keep these cans in proximity to the other person, the more they appear to be theirs. Guilt by association, as they call it. In time, we not only make the claim that this collection of cans is actually theirs, but we go so far as to say that they were never ours in the first place. Suddenly, kicking the can down the road becomes an act of kicking it over onto someone else's road.

Kicking the Can Will Kick Our Can

There are implications for kicking the can down the road. Sometimes those implications are serious beyond whatever the issue was in the first place. Sometimes they're outright devastating. The reality of life is such that avoiding most things means that those things will become worse in the avoiding, not better. If we're avoiding something in the first place it's probably because it's pretty bad to begin with, otherwise we wouldn't be working so hard to avoid it. And the worse something is, the worse it's going to get if we avoid it. We add to the problem each time with avoid the problem. So, kicking the proverbial can down the road only increases in the size of the can. And when that happens there will come a time when it's too big to kick any longer.

What's Your Can?

We all have our cans. Some are small and some are anything but small. But we all have them and it would be in our best interest to be honest about them. It's time to identify our cans, as grueling and distasteful as that might be. Once we've done that, it's time to quite the kicking and start the resolving. The road to resolution might be a rough one that demands much of us, but it will not demand as much of us as it will if we keep on kicking the can. It's about being accountable. It's about being a person of integrity and intention. It's about stepping up to whatever our cans might be, purposefully reaching down, picking up the lot of them and ridding our lives of each one.

Jesus once said, "So if the Son sets you free, you will be free indeed" (John 8:36 (NIV). That is the life Jesus wants for you, a life free of cans and a road cleared. A life with no cans to kick is a life of un-littered roads that grant us unobstructed passage to vast horizons. And it would seem that a litter free road would be a rather nice one to travel. It might be wise to consider adopting a can free life and giving up a kicking career.

Chapter Thirteen
Conscience or Convenience
The Relentless Voice in Our Head

"…by means of the hypocrisy of liars seared in their own conscience as with a branding iron…"

- 1 Timothy 4:2 (NIV)

"The torture of a bad conscience is the hell of a living soul."

- John Calvin

A conscience is that pressing sense that unerringly guides our choices and pricks us when we don't heed it's prompting. It's that mysteriously universal compass that relentlessly points true north when we don't have any idea where true north is, or when prefer to take some other direction altogether out of a sense of convenience or selfishness or fear or just plain stupidity. It's that true north that points 'true north' despite how much we turn the compass, hold it sideways, or shake it in our attempts to somehow alter how it reads the poles of our conscience.

The Resiliency of Conscience

However, a conscience won't bend, it won't be compromised, it's impermeable in the face of smooth talk, and it listlessly blows off the most compelling justifications as pithy nonsense. It refuses to be unsullied by selfishness, it won't succumb to the flighty arguments of politically correct pabulum, it won't sell itself out to the most convincing of arguments, and it can't be bribed. It will effortlessly sluff off the most smoothly crafted rationalizations despite how ingenious or intense our crafting of them has been.

If indeed our conscience does compromise itself in the face of any of these, we can be assured that it's no longer our conscience that we're hearing. There are many lesser voices that speak a language of compromise. And even though none of these are as piercing, as pure, and as compelling as our conscience, that does not mean that we do not pay ready attention to them.

The Demands of Our Conscience

A conscience can be very demanding. It can be life-altering if heeded and life-halting if ignored. It can generate a deep sense of well-being and rightness when we obey it. Likewise, it can infect us with a gnawing sense of uncertainty and guilt when we disregard it. It can save us if we let it and bless us if we bend to it. However, we will die in the rejection of it and be cursed if we bow to the lesser things that would have us bow to them.

More times than we can count we end up in places wondering how in the world we got there. We got there (wherever there is) simply because we crafted our 'today' from the choices that we made 'yesterday.' Each day we set a trajectory that will reflect the beliefs and values from which (and by which) we set that trajectory. And if we dare to understand this reality, the answer as to why we repeatedly end up in less than savory places is quite easily solved by realizing that the trajectory to this less than appealing place was determined by the degree to which we adhered to or rejected our conscience.

Ignoring Our Conscience

Because our conscience is immovable, our only choice to deal with it when we don't like it is to either ignore it or aggressively edit it. Despite the priceless nature of our conscience, we can most certainly snub it. It's utterly amazing that something so precious won't demand that we give it audience, and that it will allow us to discard it if we fall to such foolishness.

Our conscience will not force itself upon us or demands its way with us. It will not press itself to the forefront or raise its voice over the swarming chorus of other voices that incessantly call us to lesser things. Our conscience is precious beyond understanding and powerful beyond words to describe. Yet truly great power is always recognized by the willingness of that which is powerful to restrain its power even at great cost to itself. Such is God and such is the conscience that He has generously gifted us with.

Our conscience graciously makes itself available to us, but it will move into the background if we deny its voice. Therein lays the terribly frightening reality of it all. If we turn a deaf ear to our conscience, its voice will become ever smaller and ever thinner. In time it can become such a whisper-thin murmuring that we can't even make it out anymore. And left to our own devices or having fallen prey to the devices of these lesser voices, our trajectory is set, the course is plotted, and we find ourselves hurdling to imminent destruction.

Constructing a Conscience of Convenience

We have a deeply core sense that we must have some sort of opinion. We have to have some guiding function of some sort, regardless of where we get it from or how well it might work for us. We need some principle of some sort that informs our decisions so that we're not informed. We don't do well simply meandering through life without some ethic, or presumed sense of morality, or cultural mandate, or familial tradition that guides us. We have to hold onto something that guides (or possibly drives) our decisions…some compass regardless of its design or origins. And while we often don't sufficiently consider the compass itself or its potentially dubious origins, we're holding onto something because the nature of this existence demands it.

Without an internal compass of some sort, our decisions become chaotically disjointed and our direction as dictated by those decisions leads us to a life of meandering meaninglessness. We need something that tells us that we're not alone when we're standing at some crossroads making potentially life-altering decisions. That there is a comforting partnership that will provide a guiding function when the questions are large, and thc challenges are larger. Sometimes we want that 'something' so that should things go terribly wrong, we have a ready place to dump the blame. In essence, we have a means of escape where we can conveniently save face. Either way, each of us has something that we would describe as our belief system, or our moral guidelines, or our established standards that provide us that guiding function.

It seems that we all have a deeply inbred conscience that is a core part of our shared humanity. Yet too often we ignore those belief systems or morals. While our conscience is typically a highly reliable compass, it might direct us away from what we want, or direct us to what we don't want. It might get in our way, or spoil our fun, or make us look the fool, or delay our gratification, or place us someplace other than where some politically correct position says that we should be. Our conscience might set us apart from the very crowd that we so desperately want to be a part of, or call some cherished goal into question, or prompt us to repent of choices that we'd prefer to ignore.

However, because we need some guiding principle, we subsequently borrow or manufacture a fresh set of beliefs or morals or principles that more readily accommodate our agendas. We want user-friendly convictions. We want a convenient conscience. We prefer to justify what we want rather than evaluate the wisdom in the getting. We're big on rationalization and we're schooled in justification. And if our conscience gets in the way of our cherished goals, or if it creates an unsettling disturbance within us in the pursuit of them, we'll readily modify or create a new conscience. And quite often, these are borrowed or manufactured because we didn't like what our conscience was telling us, or it didn't work all that well within our social group, or it didn't support our cultural agenda, or it got in the way of our greed, or for a million assorted reasons it was just plain irritating.

Borrowed

Borrowing a belief system or set of morals is frighteningly easy simply because there are so many of them available to choose from. The options appear utterly endless. We live in a culture that wants to press questionable agendas, or justify spurious actions, or grant permission to choices that would otherwise be less than acceptable. To circumvent any objections and release us from the irritating pangs of guilt, there are an innumerable array of entities and countless causes that have crafted their own beliefs and morals so as to grant themselves unbridled permission to proceed in whatever manner they choose. Subsequently, the selections are incredibly innumerable and at times quite tantalizing. Yet, what we're selecting are justifications for our agendas rather than cultivating core principles by which to live our lives.

Created

Or we take a bit of license and we create our own beliefs and morals. We figure that we'll take our conscience, and we'll update it just a bit. We shave off the demanding corners so that it's a bit more palatable and a whole lot more comfortable. We edit it sufficiently so that it doesn't interfere with our cherished agendas. We do a bit of nip-and-tuck it so that it gives us permission to do what it didn't give us permission to do before we rigorously applied our justifying scalpel to it. We can become rather creative and somewhat innovative so that the finished product has a perceived sense of morality while granting us the fullest permission to function as we please. And despite our perceptions to the contrary, all we've done is to create justifications for our agendas rather than cultivate core principles by which to live our lives.

Conscience or Convenience?

And so, the main question is, will we live guided by our conscience or compelled by convenience? Will we fall to lesser things because they give us permission to live for lesser things? Will we walk the path of compromise to the cliff of convenience, or will we recognize that any path not informed by conscience will always lead to a cliff?

The trajectory of these two choices is entirely different and the destinations that they lead us to are likely to be diametrically opposed. More times than we can count we end up in places wondering how in the world we got there. Such a mystery is quite easily solved by simply realizing that the trajectory to these less than appealing places was determined by the degree to which we adhered to or rejected our conscience or opted for convenience. Since that is clearly the case, we'd be quite wise to attend to that inner voice, whether we find it appealing or whether we find it utterly irritating. It would behoove us to listen to our conscience whether it grants us what we want or whether it withholds everything that we want. For where we end up and the nature of the trajectory that we are on will be dictated by that incredibly important choice.

Chapter Fourteen
Convictions
The Lack Thereof

"But if serving the LORD seems undesirable to you, then choose for yourselves this day whom you will serve, whether the gods your forefathers served beyond the River, or the gods of the Amorites, in whose land you are living. But as for me and my household, we will serve the LORD."

- Joshua 24:15 (NIV)

"Never for the sake of peace and quiet deny our convictions."

- Dag Hammarskjold

We live in a world spiraling in a confounding kaleidoscopic of shoddy opinions, self-serving biases, vacillating cultural mandates, clarion calls for whatever politically correct notion might be trending at the moment, and the elusive lure of all thing's vogue and trendy. We're frantically chasing some perpetually shifting norm that's nothing of a norm but everything of a culture hell-bent on justifying everything that it wishes to justify. It is the incendiary concoction of instant-gratification, rogue entitlement, rights unrestrained by reason, liberties bled of logic, and greed victimizing both those who unleashed it as well as those that it was unleashed upon.

Godly values are no longer the premise by which we

shape our life or our culture. Rather, they have become the pitifully abhorrent and wholly illegitimate obstacle to our desires. We have labeled them as some dusty set of antiquated ideals that we must dutifully purge ourselves of. These ideals served a generation that lived out its days in the backwaters of an ignorance fed comatose by intellectual stupor and ill-informed beliefs. Therefore, their value rests solely in their removal so that hitherto unexplored horizons can be freely traversed. The problem is that our culture has yet to discern a horizon from a cliff, and we as Christians seem to have lost that discernment as well.

We have defined 'progressive' as being free of any restraint that might impede our ability to stoke the flames of our passions or chase after the hem of our perversions. Right and wrong have become defined by personal or cultural preferences that shift as the winds on uncertain seas. Simply having the desire for something now renders both the thing and the desire as 'right.' External values that are timeless have been replaced by internal desires that change in no time. It is the elevation of the self at the destruction of the self.

Convictions
What They Are

Convictions born of shifting opinions, tainted biases, cultural mandates, politically correct notions, and all things vogue and trendy are not convictions. Their sole focus is a stringent uniformity to a larger social agenda. As such, these agendas do not adhere to something bigger than themselves in order to keep themselves from falling prey to themselves. There are a millions of minuscule compasses all pointing in different directions that pull the culture apart as people scurry to chase whatever 'north' their particular compass happens to be pointing to.

We would be wise to remember that an agenda based on 'self' is destined to consume the very 'self' that the agenda is seeking to liberate. A compass that is calibrated to point at what we want, rather than what we need will destroy us. And in a culture violently consuming itself, such crazed thinking will only serve to hasten that death. Therefore, the need for the bold reclamation and clear declaration of Godly convictions becomes increasingly obvious and ever pressing.

Godly Convictions

Godly convictions give no voice, much less any space to these lesser things, for these lesser things are contaminated by the selfish agendas that constructed them. Godly convictions recognize that the convictions that save us or not those that gratify us. The convictions that keep us standing upright, living upright, as well as moving both 'up' and 'right' must be free of the meddling's of men and the lesser passions that drive that meddling.

Convictions are grounded in principles irrefutably larger and infinitely bigger than the grubby pabulum of selfish mandates and self-serving trends. Convictions rest in things that supersede our waffling culture, and they are sustained by things that will exist long after that culture finds its demise at the hands of the lesser things that the culture squandered its life for.

Convictions that hold us back from our own demise and raise us to our greatest potential cannot be penned by men who assume that our own demise is not getting what we want, (when that is the sure and certain course of our demise). Godly convictions do not give us what we want, but they provide us everything that we need. And until we look past our greed and understand that what we 'need' is actually what we need to 'want', we will craft convictions that give us permission to discount convictions.

The Commitment to and the Cost of Convictions

Convictions are those things that we will stand on even when the culture exerts phenomenal effort to have us stand-down. We would rather die by our convictions than dic by the dying culture that defies them. They are the timeless values that did not somehow exhaust their time in some other time because their essence is entirely unbound by time. They are life. They are wisdom. They are stability and bold assurance. They are unmoved and immovable even when everything else is moving. They are steadfastly consistent, entirely unintimidated, and ever superior. They are the uncompromising and irrefutable foundation of every shred of our existence. They are the ingeniously created essence of everything that we need to live out this existence with abundance, confidence and victory. And because they are all of these things, we would rather die by our convictions than die by the dying culture that defies them.

Convictions Are Not Convenient

However, convictions are not convenient. Neither are they popular. They are not vogue nor are they trendy, for a culture bent on satiating its own appetites will find nothing vogue or trendy that does not feed it in the way that it demands to be fed. Convictions are based on what is right, not on what is convenient. They are embedded in principles that are eternally sustained and are not fazed by our rejection of them. They are stalwart, sturdy regardless of the number of enemies brought against them, and invincible in the face of lesser arguments despite how well articulated and crafty they might be. They do not fall to lesser arguments, and their power is not reduced by their lack of popularity (for it is in such hostile environments that they thrive). Their untainted relevance renders everything irrelevant that would claim the same of these convictions.

Therefore, convictions call us to endure ridicule because they are likely to be branded as intolerant, ignorantly constrictive and uninformed as held against the permissive liberties that our culture has ascribed as its due. They are demanding as they call us apart from everything that they are not, which means that in today's culture we may find ourselves abjectly alone at times and often isolated in that loneliness. They recognize that the call to great things is often the call to great pain, and therefore convictions hold no illusion about that to which they call us. Yet, to abandon our convictions is to incur a far greater pain.

The Importance of Standing

Convictions are the principles that God has woven into and throughout the whole of this existence in order to preserve and perpetuate that very existence. Therefore, they are set against all of that which seeks to destroy this existence. They are what feeds a dying world and offsets the sin that would consume it in order to hasten that death. At times they are by nature contrary to everything that we want, but they are perfectly crafted to perpetuate everything that we need. We would be wise to remember that Godly convictions are our liberties, for they safeguard us against all the lesser things that would seek to destroy us, including ourselves. And if our culture is to survive, we must rigorously stand on these convictions in the face of a culture pounding out ever-shifting convictions that are in fact self-destructive agendas.

Convicting Thoughts

Could it be that we are the generation that is living out its days in the backwaters of an ignorance fed comatose by intellectual stupor? Are we that which we have declared others to be in order to give ourselves permission to be what we should not be? Are the disjointed efforts of opinions, biases, cultural mandates, politically correct notions, and all things vogue and trendy an effort to write ourselves sweeping permission to justify sweeping behaviors that will in time sweep us away? As the Christian community living out its faith in a roiling culture, have we become principally unprincipled because we have fallen in step with a rogue humanity blindly bent on a self-actualization that is, in fact, blind self-destruction?

And if this is so, are we ready to throw off selfish agendas for timeless principles so that we might save ourselves from ourselves? Are we ready to stand on Godly convictions and refuse to wallow in culturally provoked trends? As the body of Christ, do we definitively divorce ourselves from the cultural prose and the self-satiating policies that have seeped into the soul of the Christian community? Do we rid ourselves of the 'cultural Christianity' that has tamed our faith and muted our message? Do we commit to live as members of an eternal kingdom, rather than as citizens in a temporal one? Will we live out our convictions in broad daylight so that they will penetrate the building darkness? Will we pick up our Bibles, get on our knees, and stand on our faith in a culture that will work to stand on us? Will we? Because if we do, we can change everything because that's what convictions do.

Chapter Fifteen
To Decide or Not to Decide
The Impact

"If any of you lacks wisdom, let him ask God, who gives generously to all without reproach, and it will be given him.'

- James 1:5 (NIV)

"In any moment of decision, the best thing you can do is the right thing, the next best thing is the wrong thing, and the worst thing you can do is nothing."

- Theodore Roosevelt

Decisions. Life is quite literally jam-packed with them. We make them all of the time; literally one after another after another. Hardly a single minute passes where we're not thinking through and making some sort of decision. Some decisions are huge and sweeping, amply possessing both the power and scope to impact our lives for the rest of our lives. Others are small and passively demur, doing little more than impacting the few brief moments that follow the decision.

Some decisions follow a predictable and patently obvious course, being crisply and closely dictated by the laws of nature, or cultural expectations, or a set of values, or the tutelage of a mentor, or an established tradition of some sort. These decisions are frequently more reflexive than thoughtful as they have naturally established boundaries that provide an automatic guiding function. Other more complex and intricate decisions may not as easily adhere to such established boundaries, demanding degrees of accommodation, various levels of modification, or some measure of generous reassessment that calls on reasoning, thought processes and wisdom rarely accessed.

Some decisions are repetitive, demanding that we make them every day so that they become less decisions and more habits. Some are decisions around legitimate things (that by virtue of their legitimacy) deserve a decision, as well as the time and the energy that it takes us to make a decision. Others are decisions that we are obligated to make regarding things that shouldn't have happened in the first place (and whose legitimacy is all but absent) forcing us to waste our time and energy. Regardless, we all make all kinds of decisions for all kinds of reasons. And we make tons of them.

Missing the Impact

In whatever way decisions come, we make so many decisions that they can become reflexively habitual. And in becoming habitual, we often pay them little mind. Or we may view decisions as part of a general progression that serves only to move us to the next place. Therefore, it is our sense, either conscious or unconscious, that both the value and the impact of the decision ceases to exist at the point that it has moved us to that next place. Or at times we may view decisions as necessary evils, and we therefore make them so as to get them off of our backs. Once we have removed ourselves from them or them from us, we leave them behind with little thought as to what impact they might have now that they are behind us. Or we may be forced to make decisions we'd prefer not to make and therefore we readily defer any negative consequences because circumstances or situations forced us to make decisions that we would have not otherwise made.

In whatever way we do it, we somehow dispose of decisions as some sort of consumed article bereft of life and wholly expended because they have served their purpose. We errantly assume them to be spent because they have achieved their goal, or we imagine them neutralized because the task for which they were determined has been completed. Yet, decisions remain very much alive as do the repercussions of them.

The Impact Outside of the Decision

Regardless of the manner in which they are made, we often make decisions not nearly comprehending the full impact of the decision beyond the decision. Too often decisions are made for the sole purpose of making the decision and in making the decision, bringing whatever the situation is to a conclusion. It's checking something off of our list rather than checking what it might do to our lives. We may consider the long-term implications, but we typically do so as they apply directly to the decision. As such, the residue of each decision remains, being compounded by all of the decisions that follow. And in time, we are left to make a decision about the impact of all of the decisions that we've made.

Seldom do we consider the broad and far-reaching implications that lay out beyond the singular decision and the situation that prompted the decision. We take too little time to realize that the biggest and most potent impact of our decisions are often not related to the decisions themselves or the situations that demanded those decisions. It seldom dawns on us that a decision holds to no walls, has no boundaries, and it will linger in ways both passive and bold long after the decision has been rendered. We forget that a decision is not consumed and spent as it is applied to the situation that we made the decision for. Rather, each decision lingers. Each decision spends ripples into the future which can eventually create regret in the past within which the decision was made.

The biggest impact of any decision is often the repercussions felt outside and far beyond those situations and corresponding decisions. Life is not so rigidly cloistered as to be confined to a single space or a solitary place. Such is the case with every decision that we render. In fact, it is often the case that others entirely unassociated with our decisions can be dramatically impacted by our decisions without knowing who or what or where the repercussions came from. Situations that seem entirely unrelated and that lie so far out on the horizon of life that we can't even see them from our vantage point can be unalterably effected. Even time itself can be impacted for all time. Eons after the decisions are made and the situations that demanded them have fallen deep into the catacombs of history, the implications of our decisions can remain potent and impactful.

Little do we realize that decisions made over situations now long dead may in fact demand other decisions that would be entirely unnecessary and wholly irrelevant if more care had been taken in making the original decisions in the first place. We so myopically focus on the moment, the perceived needs of the moment, and our desire to rid ourselves of some problem that we render decisions without considering the frequently cataclysmic implications of those decisions for the future. Indeed, do we dare to understand the power and reach of our decisions, and out of that understanding do we begin to approach each decision with much more caution and much less ambivalence?

Decisions to Thwart Decisions

Often, we have to make decisions to thwart previously made decisions, most of which were poor conceived and even more poorly executed. If we were sufficiently brave to inventory our decisions, we would quickly discover that many of our decisions were made to thwart or offset decisions that we had previously made. It may well be that the incessant busyness and increasingly demanding nature of our lives may be a direct result of all of the decisions we are currently forced to make that serve to counter other poor decisions that we made previously. It would behoove us to understand that one bad decision can spawn a hundred other decisions that serve to correct the original decision. And so, in order not to heavily frontload our future we would be wise be judicious in backloading our present.

Decisions to Deny the Impact of Our Decisions

How many times have we decided to live in denial, or immerse ourselves in exquisitely well-crafted justifications, or strategically redirect blame to innocent parties so that we can side-step the impact of our decisions? How many times do we take evasive action to steer clear of the decisions that we made in the past, as well as the decisions that we now have to make because of those decisions? How often is our decision a decision to avoid out of the misplaced belief that if you ignore something long enough or place it far enough away from ourselves that it will go away? But are we actually front-loading our lives in a manner far worse that the decisions that we are now trying to avoid?

Deciding About Our Decisions

We need to understand that in making a decision today we are creating a legacy for tomorrow, and that no decision is bound solely to the moment within which it is made and the people for whom it is made. We can touch lives that we will never meet and impact situations that we don't even know exist by a single decision that we feel is limited to the single moment that we make it in. Likewise, we cannot be so remiss as to miss the reality that what is done in the present is capable of geometrically amplifying itself in the future, leaving our lives consumed and taxed with making decisions that only serve to counter other poor decisions that we made.

Our decisions cannot be reflexively habitual. They are far more than decisions that simply serve to move us to the next place. They are not necessary evils, and we therefore make them so as to get them off of our backs. Nor are they things we'd prefer not to make and therefore we readily defer any negative consequences because circumstances or situations forced us to make decisions that we would have not otherwise made.

Instead, decisions are the shapers and crafters of our moments and our lives. They will add to our lives if we make them wisely, or they will demand everything we have to correct them if we make them poorly. They can open up a thousand doors, or they can lock a single door with a thousand locks. They can pave the way to successes unimagined, or they dissolve into trackless expanses of emotional, relational, financial and career deserts. They can breathe new life into our circumstances, or they can suck the air out of every circumstance.

And finally, they are never isolated to us alone, therefore every decision must be made understanding our responsibility to larger humanity. We must live with a respectful sense of community, even though we may not see that community in the single moment that we make that single decision. Should we persist in such terribly limited notions that have defined our poor decisions, we are certain to hurt ourselves, handicap others, and negatively load our future. We will die a death at our own hand while damaging others with that selfsame hand.

Decisions. Life is quite literally jam-packed with them. We make them all of the time; literally one after another after another. And we must learn to make them wisely.

Chapter Sixteen
The Crisis of Our Choices
Us Verses Us

"What a wretched man I am! Who will rescue me from this body that is subject to death?"

- Romans 7:24 (NIV)

"We have met the enemy and he is us."

- Walt Kelly - Pogo

We tend to rather blithely categorize times of crisis simply as happenstance occurrences that reflect the frequently volatile and somewhat unpredictable nature of life. Life happens, and sometimes it happens really hard. Through no fault of our own, we can be in the wrong place at the wrong time, even though we were doing all of the right things. We can be impacted by a series of events that did not start with us, nor will they end with us. Nonetheless, they will sweep over us as part of their devastating progression. Injustices befall us without warning.

Bosses will hoard our achievements and hail them as theirs, leaving our careers languishing in obscurity. People betray us without any inkling that they were harboring the seething hatred that they've suddenly unleashed on us. Spouses find greener pastures with lesser persons. Family members take violent stands against us as they stand in support of dysfunctional family systems. Friends step away, drawing back until they've disappeared from the landscape of our lives and our hearts. On and on it goes.

Because we tend to conceptualize crisis in this manner, we readily place times of crisis in this convenient 'us-versus-them' category. It's about some external force descending upon us with violent impunity. It's about the sky falling in on us and the bottom dropping out from under us when we had done nothing but cultivate both. It is the classic perpetrator/victim scenario. It's the aggressor violently advancing against an anointed (or not so anointed) adversary. And this framework often becomes the summation of our conceptualization of such events.

When It's Us

But what about the times when it's not 'us-verses-life?' What about the times when we've contributed to whatever's befallen us? What about the times where we've 'set' the stage with a dubious cast of characters that 'set' our lives on fire? What about the situations where we put the pieces in place that resulted in the outcome that eventually blew us to pieces? What about the steady accumulation of poor choices, misdirected actions, selfish reckonings, and wisdom recklessly redefined by whatever trend that might be deemed as "politically correct" at any given moment; all of which pressed us flat in the accumulation?

What about the little things that we thought didn't matter? What about those small errors, those tiny slips, those momentary lapses? What about those moments when we turned away, walked away, or shied away from things that maybe we shouldn't have? Or, what about the larger choices? What about the missteps, the misinformation, and the mismanagement that caused us to miss the mark? What about the times when it was 'us-verses-us?' How often are we the culprit, or we're at least culpable, or we're in cahoots with whatever or whoever came after us? What about the times when it's us?

Honest with Ourselves

Is the crisis of our choices really a crisis of character? Do we need to step back from the ready-made template of 'us-versus-them' and quit using that rubric with such liberality? Do we need to see our own hand in things, and be honest about the fingerprints that we've left strewn across some of our most devastating moments? Our greatest advances are made when we acknowledge our greatest failures. It is not in ignoring our culpability that we find solace or refuge. It's in acknowledging our role that we find freedom, we discover solutions, and we experience healing. It's being honest about the fact that 'us-verses-us' may explain some of our greatest tragedies and free us from some of our greatest pain.

The Reality of Consequences

When we think about our role in things, do we actually think that we can live without consequences? Do we believe that we have that kind of liberty? Is it our sense that we can freely make choices that will serve us in whatever way we want them to serve us without simultaneously constructing the consequences that will upend us? Is our sense of entitlement so deeply embossed in our heads that we have fallen for the belief that we can do what we want and that our want of something is sufficient to negate the consequences of getting whatever that is?

In other words, have we constructed some justifying framework that makes 'us-verses-us' permissible? Have we made it okay to be our own worst enemy? Or have we freed ourselves of the consequences of doing so to the point that we actually appear to be the victims? Do we become the victim of consequences that we have justified away, therefore leaving us convinced that because we've actually experienced some sort of consequence our misfortune must be due to someone else?

Absolutes

Is life of our own constructs or is there a greater construct that will experience upheaval and fracturing if we press it? Are there a set of principles set into, under and all around this existence of ours that will not be tampered with? Are there rigorous and immovable fundamentals to life that we've recklessly labeled as the sad rubrics pounded out on the pulpits of religious fanatics?

And is there another set of opposing ethics held by sorry souls who believe that taking license with ethics in order to seize some grand adventure justifies the taking? Are these morals given legitimacy by those who believe that the morality of today must be recast in order to seize the opportunities of tomorrow? Or is there a stalwart standard that is immovable because the basis of all existence rests squarely upon it?

The Consequence of Messing with Absolutes

And if so, what are the consequences of incessantly hammering all around the foundation of such a standard, or tediously scribbling endless essays to redefine it, or building massive ramparts to breech it, or attempting to ignore it altogether because its permanence leaves us with no other reasonable option? What are the consequences?

As for consequences, there are many. Some we see as consequences because they clearly present themselves as such. Others we don't recognize as consequences because we have no other alternative than to attribute them to something else so that the deviant nature of our agendas are not exposed as deviant. And some we ignore until we can't. But there are consequences. Many of them. And when those consequences descend in whatever manner they do, where do we place the blame? Who do we hold responsible? To where do we point our finger in both anger and disgust?

Us-Verses-Us

When the consequences blow cold and turn things dark, we set out on this mad hunt for the perpetrator of whatever's befallen us. And how many times have we gone in search of some enemy only to find ourselves? How many times is the finger pointing back at us with an anger and disgust magnified beyond our ability to endure because in the finger-pointing we've discovered that it's 'us-verses-us.' To our own dismay and incessant denial, how many times are we standing at the bottom of this massive hole finding that the shovel is in our own hands and it's caked with dirt and marked with our fingerprints? How many times do we have a smoking gun in one hand, a fistful of ammunition in the other, and a couple of other guns sitting around just waiting to be used? How many times is it 'us-verses-us?'

This is not to say that every crisis that slams itself into our lives and broadsides our souls is a product of our choices. That would be far too naïve. But many are. Probably too many.

What to Do?

And so, when the torrent of some crisis rains into our lives, we might be wise to ask how much of this is our doing? Have we contributed to whatever's befallen us? Did our decisions set the stage? Have our attempts to recast our morality put the pieces in place that eventually blew us to pieces? Has the steady accumulation of poor choices, misdirected actions, selfish reckonings, and wisdom recklessly redefined by whatever trend that's deemed to be "politically correct" at any given moment done us in? Have we searched for the enemy and in doing so we find ourselves at every turn? Is it 'us-verses-us?'

Again, not every crisis is of our doing. Nonetheless, crisis is a time of re-evaluation. It's a time to sit back, place aside everything that we think we want and replace that with what we should want. It is a time to recognize that we can play with morality, we can tinker with ethics, we can grant ourselves license to do whatever we want, we can entitle ourselves to being entitled, and we can align ourselves with whatever is 'correct' at whatever moment we happen to find ourselves in. However, we might want to consider the depth of the hole that we're in and how much the gun is smoking. We might want to ask ourselves a whole lot of questions that we really don't want to ask ourselves. But those are often the best questions to ask, unless you enjoy living a life of 'you-verses-you.'

Chapter Seventeen
Assumptions
Agendas and Danger

"The Israelites sampled their provisions but did not inquire of the LORD."

- Joshua 9:14 (NIV)

"The explanation requiring the fewest assumptions is most likely to be correct."

- Franciscan friar William of Ockham

Most of us are quite familiar with the old saying about 'assuming.' In fact, the rather biting truth about that saying has likely bitten us more than once and we probably have the scars to prove it. Yet despite this rather endearing bit of truth (as well as the scars that we carry around with us that evidence it as true), we nonetheless go through life making a sizeable number of assumptions that have a sizeable impact. As Denis Waitley wrote, "You must stick to your convictions, but be ready to abandon your assumptions." Sadly, we regularly confuse the two, living in the laziness of assumptions sloppily labeled as convictions.

What Are Assumptions?

Assumptions are cursory conclusions that are arrived at based on an amalgamation of baser and less than robust thought processes. These thought processes are typically fouled by twisting biases, dictated by rogue stereotypes, fed by various rumors, and seasoned by cultural prejudices among other things. We tend to grab these somewhat spurious thought processes, toss them together and throw out whatever pops out. And because this is frequently the course by which our assumptions are created, we would be entirely free of assumption to state that assumptions are quite flawed.

Sometimes assumptions are borne of laziness. It's easier to assign stereotypes or let biases do the talking. We can fall back on what everyone else has said, or let our preconceived ideas win the day. We can employ a handful of previously constructed paradigms that we can force-fit with a bit of nip-and-tuck accompanied with some not-so-slight pressure applied around the edges. These allow us to make assumptions utilizing very little time or energy.

However, this process of developing assumptions appears to be missed or justified due to the fact that over time we completely confuse these tainted thought processes with things such as cultured wisdom, a penetrating discernment, tested intuition, and a refined acumen. And because we assume that these rather regal thought-processes are what has crafted our perspectives and subsequently driven our decisions, we assume that we're not assuming, which in and of itself is a terribly flawed assumption. We are then left believing that we have engaged in a thought process of the most responsible sort when we have likely engaged in assumptions of the most irresponsible sort.

Agendas as the Birthplace of Assumptions

Often at the core of our assumptions rests our

agendas. Our agendas dictate what we want life to look like, with the equally potent agenda of what we want ourselves to look like. We then develop a composite collection of assorted assumptions that serve to support these agendas. We create tidy boxes that we assume everything should neatly fit into. We construct pre-packaged biases that we assume will easily and conveniently categorize everyone's behaviors. We tediously outline some pre-determined pecking order that we assume will allow us to quickly size-up and tidily pigeon-hole everybody that we meet. We develop 'righteous' goals that we assume are wholly committed to the betterment of man, even if most of the unfortunate people that we run into lack the vision to grasp that fact.

And it is our agenda of what we want life to look like and what we want ourselves to look like (whatever all of this might be) that births, guides and subsequently feeds these various assumptions. Through this nurturing process we gradually legitimize these assumptions through adherence to them over time, our continual refinement of them, frequent academic or informational investigation that is often biased in the direction of the assumption, and a myopic evolution where in time we can see nothing else but these assumptions. And because we have slowly legitimized these assumptions through this unconscious thought process, in our minds they gradually move from opinion to fact.

Once we've assumed that these assumptions are fact, we are then endowed with some sort of card-carrying card-blank permission to liberally dispense them without the kind of cautious contemplation that opinion might demand of us. And now we're about the rather frightening business of dispensing our assumptions disguised as fact, which does not and cannot make our assumptions any less than assumptions, despite our assumptions to the contrary. Because we've legitimized our agendas by converting our assumptions to facts, we become dangerous. And that danger is no assumption.

The Danger

We're not likely to question our agendas because they have become facts. But more fundamental than that, we're not likely to question them because in doing so we would have to question the sum total of our agendas. Questioning our agendas would likely mean that we would have to question the foundational principles upon which we've built the entirety of our lives. It means that we would be forced to face the world as it is, not as we would like it to be. More problematic than that, that means that we would have to face ourselves as who we actually are, rather than who or what we'd like to be. And so, we adamantly adhere to our assumptions because they support the agendas that we are far too insecure and infinitely too frightened to question.

We are then forced to live in a world that we're really not living in, being people that we are not, making other people out to be what they're not, seeing situations as something other than what they really are, and missing the whole of life through the whole process. Because we throw around assumptions based on our agendas, we can't change anything because we don't have an accurate understanding of what we're changing or if it really needs to be changed at all. We become bellicose and belligerent, thinking that we have all the answers to all the questions if people would just be smart enough to do what we say. We can alienate relationships, damage lives, run rogue through organizations, trample trust, and stomp on the best of intentions all based on errant assumptions driven by our selfish agendas that we've labeled as facts and are too fearful to see as anything but facts.

And So, What to Do

First, Am I So Weak?

I must first ask if I am so weak that I can only survive by creating agendas that protect me from the real world and make me something other than what I am. Do I perceive myself as so inadequate or ill-prepared that I must avoid the real world and my real self in order to live out even the most marginal existence? Will I allow my assumptions to protect me from the realities of a world that they can't protect me from anyway? Am I so weak that I will forfeit life in the avoidance of it? If I look closely, this need not be the case.

Second, Will I Be a Champion?

Second, I must begin to believe that the real world is in reality begging to be changed if someone brave enough would step up and do it. The world isn't looking for a hero. It's looking for ordinary people who are willing to do something extraordinary, for the world can relate to that and it can replicate that. While the world is a tough place, the world is also a hurting place. It is the same with us. The world out there, as well as the world within us is looking for champions that would cause us to believe that it can be different. That it can be changed. That it doesn't have to be this way. If we look closely, we will soon realize that we can be that champion.

Third, Am I Willing to Abandon My Assumptions?

Third, I must abandon all assumptions, despite how tantalizing and comforting and soothing they might be. The rationale for such a bold course of action lies in understanding the inherently flawed nature of assumptions, and that such flaws will always do more damage than good. It's understanding that assumptions degrade, diminish, and can destroy those who we are making assumptions about. They will block our ability to understand a world that needs someone to understand it in order to change it. No one wins, and to some degree everyone dies. And with a cost that enormous, are we willing to abandon our assumptions?

Fourth, Crafting Agendas Based on the Best Interest of Others

Fourth, I must craft agendas not based on my agendas. I must look at the reality of the world around me and craft agendas that are based on the best interest of that world that I see around me. What does the world need? What does my neighbor need? How about the person in front of me in line at the grocery? How about the billions of people I will never meet as well as the thousands that I will? This is nothing less than sacrificing our lives for the betterment of others, understanding that such an action may not better our lives, but they may better someone else's. Yet, it is in the price paid for others that I discover the most profound growth.

Finally, I Must Not Borrow the Assumptions of Others

Finally, I must not let the assumptions of others become my assumptions. I must not let their assumptions creep into my thinking or, let mine creep into theirs. I must be willing to see the world as the world is, despite the frequently frightening nature of such an action. While it would be significantly easier to fall in step with others and be embraced by them as I embrace their agendas, I must be willing to court rejection if that be the price of refusing the assumptions of others.

Not an Assumption

Diligently adhere to these and your life will change. It will clean the lens of your soul, wipe clean the grime of your conscience, and set you face-to-face with a world that's dying to be seen and accepted for what it is. For it is in seeing the world as it is that we begin to develop a vision of what it can be. And you can be assured that this is not an assumption.

Chapter Eighteen
Habit
Servant or Dictator

"… not giving up meeting together, as some are in the habit of doing, but encouraging one another—and all the more as you see the Day approaching."

- Hebrews 10:25 (NIV)

"The chains of habit are too weak to be felt until they are too strong to be broken."

- Samuel Johnson

Too often we are repetitively reactionary and little more. Life becomes something more of obligatory duty rather than gifted privilege. Our days become stale, methodical routines that hammer out another empty twenty-four hours on the incessant assembly line of our lives, rather than being an astonishing adventure that could peel off in a hundred different glorious directions at any time. Living becomes banally rote, the day-in and day-out devolves to stale routine, blandness leaves us forgetting that flavor exists at all, and habit seizes the reins with both hands.

Left unchecked, habit strangles individuality by imposing sameness, and it crushes creativity by demanding adherence. Habit takes that which might have been mindful and makes it entirely mindless. It seizes the marvelous and renders it mechanical. If we are not diligently careful, habit will come to define the whole of our existence, leaving the fluid magnificence of who we are and what we could accomplish wholly dissipated in the backwash of lack-luster procedure and irreversibly dispersed in heartless protocol.

We Are Not Habit

Yet, we are exceedingly more than the bland amalgamation of habit, even though we incessantly permit its lifeless rubrics to press the life out of us. We are not the accumulated outcome of procedure, protocol or process. Those things can create effective frameworks within which we can maximize our existence, but at the point that they become our existence we have ceased to exist. We are not merely stale rubrics or sterile paradigms of our own making, or those crafted for us by our culture, our jobs, our relationships or anything else for that matter.

The outliers of our essence extend leagues out beyond our own vision, and our depth is past plumbing despite whatever discipline we might bring to the plumbing. And it is altogether impossible that the whole of this essence can be packed tidily into the asphyxiating rubric that habit constructs. Habit might indeed be unswerving and fixed, granting us a steady direction and a secure course when all becomes unsteady. Yet, given unbridled rein to freely propagate the rubrics that make habit what it is, we would die the death of character asphyxiation.

Who We Are

We are a potently composite collection of experiences, wounds, failures, successes, relationships, genetics and a wholly incalculable array of other things that press together and then settle into some sort of uniquely amalgamated compilation that makes us, us. The nature of these things and the manner in which they have each jostled for position and eventually fall into place lends us a uniqueness that sets us apart from everyone else in all of existence, while concurrently creating both adoring and sometimes irksome similarities with everyone else.

From the core of this place that makes us who we are, there emerges a refined proliferation of beliefs, values, opinions and perspectives that both drive and dictate the manner in which we engage life in ways both large and small. Indeed, this core place becomes the sturdy helm from which the ship of our lives is faithfully navigated. In time, this place becomes sagely informed, sharply intuitive and shrewdly instinctual. This proficient compilation of assets lends itself to great things beyond even the scope of our dreams and fondest aspirations.

The Helm Commandeered by Habit

However, this helm can become insidiously commandeered by habit. It is our choice to let that happen, and the choice is most often based on the curse of ease and the ignorance of our abilities. Over time, we surrender to the reflex of habit. Habit is easy. Habit demands nothing cognitively. Habit allows us to wave off responsibility and pay to attention to lesser things rather than the things that maybe we need to be paying attention to. Habit subdues mindfulness, and reflex ousts wisdom. It blunts creativity and undercuts innovation. In time we react without knowing why we're reacting, and when we reach that point, we've devolved into mindless automatons living out the staleness borne of a reactionary existence. Habit has its place, but we habitually grant it every place.

In time, habit is confused with intelligence and wisdom. We deem ourselves to be quite astute, overtly mindful, shrewdly insightful and rigorously thoughtful. We commend ourselves for the tact with which we engage life and the wisdom that exudes from us with ever increasingly depth. Yet, this is often little more than the redundant repetition of habit that we've taken for something far more than habit. We ascribe to habit brilliant ideas, epic decisions and colossal achievements that are in reality nothing of habit, all the while allowing the grander part of ourselves to atrophy in the decay of life lost.

Habit as Ease

Sadly, it seems that we create habit so that we don't have to create. Habit provides us a soulfully soothing sense that we're being amply responsible and sufficiently judicious in living out our lives while permitting us to pay as little attention as possible to the living out of our lives. It's the autopilot that we engage so that we can turn our attention to the endless other things that are pounding at the door of our lives. And once we open the door and let those things in, they fall to the death-knell of habit as well.

In time, we craft some sort of habit to deal with each of these demands as we grant them entrance into our lives. We then develop habits about developing habits, rendering each habit something of all the others before it. Habits shape habits, encourage habits, breed habits as fast as rabbits breed rabbits, and leave us listing heavy with habits until we drown in the seas of all things mechanical and rote. Our lives take on the redundancy of the habitual habits that we now apply to everything. Soon, staleness becomes our lot, and the apathy of redundancy becomes our trademark. Despite the dankness of it all it is easy, and the habit of ease repeated habitually is the pallor of death.

The Habit of Getting Out of Habit

There might be a bit of wisdom in doing a little, or possibly a lot of introspective inventorying in order to determine the extent to which the decay of habit has infiltrated the fabric of our lives. We can fall to the mindless repetition of habit and live out our lives as a series of encoded reflexes rather than digging down, getting our hands marvelously dirty, and being mindfully engaged in a grand adventure that we're on the verge of throwing away. We can ferret out the scourge of ease and confront the debilitating messages that ease has bribed us with. We can get into the habit of getting out of the habit.

Getting into the habit of getting out of the habit means that we need to be brutally honest with ourselves. Ferreting our habit can be overtly frightening due to the fact that it is often habit that has created the very framework that we've used to bind our lives together. It becomes the bailing wire that's holding the whole assorted mess together. We fear that abandoning habit will cause our worlds to implode beyond recognition or hope of recovery.

Habit is the tightly cinching framework that binds the precarious parts of our lives together in a manner that allows our lives to hold together when life assails us. Habit retains a soothing familiarity when all becomes jarringly unfamiliar. Indeed, it may restrain us from great things at times, but in excess it also insulates us from falling into terrible things. It is a sure course when the course to adventure is unsure (for if anything is sure, it is not adventure). Habit is a certain passage that is certain to keep us safe, but too much of it is certain to keep us safely at a distance from greatness and goals both grand and glorious.

The Benefit of Habit

It is both responsible and important to point out that habit has an important and terribly critical place in our lives. Habit provides consistency to areas of our lives while we concurrently push out into other areas that have yet to be consistent or may never be consistent. They can be a series of strategic boundaries that intentionally set the stage for us to safely step outside of those boundaries to new ones. Habits can keep rather rogue and rowdy behaviors in check while giving more responsible behaviors ample room to flourish and grow. They can provide a framework until those parts of lives have matured sufficiently to stand on their own.

Yet, this brand of 'habit' is carefully crafted of wisdom, sown supple with flexibility, evenly tempered by vision, and held to places where it is needed while being withheld from places where it is not. These kinds of habits are designed to pave the way for the next step rather than insulating us from the next step. They are the progressive not regressive. Visionary and not visually blind. Progressive habits frame our lives to advance our lives for the whole of our lives. And it is these kinds of habits that will habitually keep us from the death knell of destructive habits.

We need to get into the habit of recognizing our habits. Once we have, we need to develop the habit of evaluating our habits even though we have a habit of not doing so. We need to make certain that they serve us, but not starve us. And it is this piercing acumen that will allow us to bend habit so that it does not bend us and become our death knell.

Chapter Nineteen
Bobbing and Weaving
The Dance of Justification and Rationalization

"The man said, 'The woman you put here with me—she gave me some fruit from the tree, and I ate it.' Then the LORD God said to the woman, 'What is this you have done?' The woman said, 'The serpent deceived me, and I ate.'"

- Genesis 3:12-13 (NIV)

"We first crush people to the earth, and then claim the right of trampling on them forever, because they are prostrate."

- Lydia Maria Child

We're not all too bad at bobbing and weaving. We're pretty good at side-stepping and side-lining issues. We're quite adept at cutting and spinning, doing a bit of fanciful dodging, as well as deftly running the obstacle course without getting so much as a scratch on us. We've learned to see things coming from a long way away, and we've figured out how to duck and cover with rather amazing agility so that all that stuff rolls right by us without so much as a scratch. We get the game, we get the need to master the game, we get the need to succeed at the game, we get gamey at playing the game, and we bob and weave in order to win the game.

The Art of Bobbing and Weaving

However you want to visualize it, we have a way of trying to wriggle around or weasel our way out of a whole array of things as a critical part of playing the game. It seems that our first reaction to being confronted or being called on the carpet is to rapidly figure out a series of shrewd moves to deftly dance around the carpet. We've developed an engrained habitual nature where our first reflex is to deflect whatever's been pointed at us or placed on us. Our initial intent is to figure how we get out of this, whatever this might happen to be. We deflect, we project, we place blame, we accuse, we divert, and we bob and weave.

The Curse of Accountability

What we typically don't do is to evaluate our culpability. That doesn't set all that well with us. Our mindset isn't naturally one of accountability where we step up, take what's ours and own it. We aren't necessarily blessed with a pressing sense of responsibility, and we're rather lax when it comes to developing an awareness that we're answerable to the choices that we've made. We aren't particularly prone to own what's ours; to settle up when we've screwed up, fess up when we've faltered, take the blame for the bombshell, or mop up when we've messed up. Rather, we bob and weave.

Instinctually, it seems that our more natural and deep-seated inclination is to try and figure out how to figure our way out of something. How do we blame it on the other guy? How do we make circumstances the culprit? How do we stage this so that we're so incredibly far from any dirt that there couldn't possibly be any on our hands? These kinds of knee-jerk reactions seem to be our first response and one to which we quite often become feverishly (even fanatically) dedicated.

In fact, sometimes we're so fixated on our efforts to avoid responsibility or circumvent taking accountability that we become blind to anything other than that. If our efforts are less than effective, we can shrewdly raise the stakes by smoothly presenting an endless array of colorful rationalizations and tediously crafting a mind-boggling and rather tangled web of sordid justifications. If that doesn't work sufficiently, we can engage in the baser practices of blame placing, counterfeiting, distorting, manipulating and straight-up lying. It's all about bobbing and weaving.

Bobbing, Weaving and Immaturity

Part of our difficulty in being responsible and accountable seems directly related our level of maturity or immaturity. There's something about immaturity that causes us to instinctively move to a rigorously defensive posture when faced with difficulties or challenges. There's an automatic and frequently overriding assumption of danger or threat that may or may not be a reality. With a singular focus on danger and not enough maturity to see anything else in order to craft any other response except self-preservation, we nervously work to protect ourselves at all costs. The actual nature of what faces us and our responsibility or accountability in it is rendered nearly invisible in light of the blindingly greater goal of protecting ourselves because that's the only agenda that we see.

Maturity is the seasoning of the person to the fullest manifestation of the person. It is the life-long and sometimes arduous process of intentionally maximizing the abilities, resources and talents of the individual so that everything that the individual is comes to its fullest fruition. Maturity is what rises out of the flames of adversity. It's the inborn product of outward experiences and inward wrestling with those experiences. Maturity is the thing born of the searing wounds, the blistered feet, the hands worn raw and bloodied, and the inescapable exhaustion of living life without working to escape the living of life. It's out of this maturity that we are able to move away from the singularly primitive response of self-preservation and entertain a host of potential options which can be infinitely more rich, expansive and enlivening. Without maturity, we bob and weave.

Bobbing, Weaving, Ethics, Value and Morals

Sometimes bobbing and weaving is nothing more than a character issue. It may rest in selfishness, self-centeredness, varying degrees of rancid narcissism, and a tainting dash of ego here and there. It's the attitude of self-that's interminable driven by such pathetic questions as "what's in my best interest, what course of action is going to get me the most of whatever it is that I want, what's going to put me in the best light or advance my agenda the furthest?" It's about the tedious strategy and the uncompromising prioritization of the brass ring that unflinchingly dictates any and all decisions.

So, if bobbing and weaving most effectively gets me to my goal, let's have at it. Conversely, if I can get some real and sustainable mileage out of the whole accountability and responsibility thing, let's be accountable and responsible. Too often the whole "what's in it for me" mentality becomes the ethic, which is not an ethic, but a selfish orientation subversively clothed in the garments of ethics.

Ethics, morals and values stand as uncompromising compasses. They are their own authorities. They are not bent by opinions, twisted by objectives, contorted by agendas or modified by any criteria. They become the goal. They are the agenda. They are the only true north in world with compasses that point in whatever direction is deemed most convenient, or most self-serving, or most politically correct. Ethics, morals and values shape everything else and are not shaped by anything else. Bobbing and weaving are methods and maneuvers by which we bend ethics, water down morals, and parse down values to serve our agendas. Without ethics, morals and values, we bob and weave.

Bobbing, Weaving and Bad Habits

In some instances, bobbing and weaving is simply the stuff of habit. Habit is simply a behavior that's become so natural that we do it without even thinking about it. The hidden danger in a habit is that, in time, the habit is presumed as normal and healthy. The behavior becomes so habitual that we never take the time to question the habit or see it as such. We never think to pause long enough and think about what we're doing and the exact nature of whatever it is that we're doing. Habit moves the action beyond evaluation. We just go about the business of doing it. And when this becomes the nature of our business, we better believe that our business will embrace a whole bunch of bobbing and weaving.

So, somewhere along the line we've picked up the habit of bobbing and weaving. Maybe it was modeled for us in the actions, behaviors and attitudes of our parents or some other adult figure. Maybe it was something that our friends did so we just melded right into their patterns as part of the gang. Maybe it was taught to us along the way by a professor, or it was pressed upon us by a boss, or it's been modeled by the incessant tides of our culture, or it's been embedded in us by some wayward mentor. Maybe it was just the course of whatever business we were in, so we presumed it as nothing more than "business." Whatever the case, it became habit, and it escaped a solely needed scrutiny. If we let it be a habit, we will bob and weave.

We are Not Designed for Bobbing and Weaving

You may want to take a personal inventory and ask what you're doing. You might have learned how to bob and weave with a superb degree of dexterity. Indeed, many of us have become quite proficient at this sordid dance. But in the bobbing and weaving, we will bob and weave past priceless opportunities for growth, precious possibilities of all kinds, and we will wholly forsake opportunities to stand up and force all lesser things to stand down. We will become terribly compromised people living out a terribly compromised life of perpetual avoidance.

We are not designed to bob and weave. This is nothing of who or what we are at our deepest core. In the frequent insanity of life and living, bobbing and weaving is our humanity repeatedly surrendering to something that's vastly inferior to us. Rather, we are undeniably designed for battle, and we are matchlessly equipped for victory in battle. We are designed to grow in the face of adversity and not in the flight from it. We are far more than bobbing and weaving would ever cause us to be. We are built to seize and not side-step. Ingrained in us is the ability to own what's ours, to settle up when we've screwed up, to fess up when we've faltered, to claim the bomb crater as ours, and to mop up when we've messed up. That is who we are. In doing these things, bobbing and weaving will find no place in a life within which it should never find a place in the first place.

Chapter Twenty
Playing the Fool
Fooling Ourselves

"The fool says in his heart, 'There is no God.'"
- Psalm 14:1 (NIV)

"The person who writes for fools is always sure of a large audience."
- Arthur Schopenhauer

We like to 'fool around' in ways that are sometimes rather humorous, quite innocent and very healthy. Sometimes we want to set the seriousness of life aside for a moment and be a bit playful. We need to remind ourselves that life is a serious venture where we've been vested with the indescribable privilege of living it in the first place. But taking it too seriously can kill the experience of living out this privilege of ours, and it can strangle the love of life that undergirds it all. Being responsible in living means living with a refined seriousness that's birthed out of this privilege we have to live life, but concurrently living a life that's thoroughly marinated with a penetrating sense of joy and a hefty sense of levity.

So, every now and then we 'fool around' as means of remembering that life is a journey stitched tight with the threads of levity and embroidered with the humor of a God who can laugh with the best of us. Life is play that reenergizes us to be able to work, and it is work that creates the space and resources to play. The interweaving of these elements elevates the laborious part of living to the point where it utterly transforms that which is intolerable into that which is amazingly appealing. This kind of living takes that which has always been imbalanced and throws it into perfect balance. And it seizes that which has been relentlessly hopeless, and it transforms it into something that is relentlessly hopeful.

We live in a world fashioned by a notoriously clever God who wove into creation all of the elements that we need to work in a manner where we can achieve the possible, and where we have the audacious ability to then step over into the impossible if we're daring enough to do that. And in the rigors of all of that, we have the ability to 'fool around' a bit and have moments of outrageous play smack-dab in the midst of that which is seriously serious.

Ingeniously, God set life up where we can work hard and play hard with neither being at the exclusion of the other. Life is not work 'or' play. Rather, it is work 'and' play, with each embraced at times and in ways that enhances the other. Not only do we have the permission to do all of that, but we also need to do all of that if indeed we are to achieve all of the great things that we are most certainly capable of achieving.

Erring in the Balance - Play

There's something within us that understands all of this at some fundamental level. But it seems that we're rarely able to understand it sufficiently enough to articulate it, much less work it out in some meaningful kind of way. We sense there to be some rather mysterious core elements in life that if discovered and then blended correctly will allow us to live with a whole lot more vigor and meaning and purpose and vitality. There are some key ingredients that are a key part of the concoction of life that if mixed together in some sort of appropriate proportion will pop the lid off of life and release us to authentic life and living. At some level we all know that, but we don't know exactly how that all works.

And so, we seek all of that out in whatever way we seek all of it out. It's something akin to baking without a recipe where we're not all that certain as to what the ingredients actually are, or how much of them we actually use. And if we somehow get somewhere close to whatever they are, we're still not all that certain of how to correctly mix them and then properly bake them anyway.

Heavy on Play

And in trying to figure all of this out as we live out our lives, we seem to fall rather heavily on the play side of things. We load up the recipe of life with a heavy dose of play, or so it seems. It seems that we tend to emphasize the whole idea of play as it appears to be a whole lot more fun, and it's not top-heavy with all the onerous things that the work side seems straddled with. It's light and airy when work is not. It only asks that we have fun when work demands that we be productive. Play is far more appealing and far less repelling. And so, we seem to load up on it a bit.

Light on Play

Or there are those of us who are rather stingy with the whole 'plaything.' We sprinkle in a slightly slight pinch of play because we see it as something that really doesn't contribute to our goals, so we don't want too much of it. Play is a diversion that's counterproductive. Its time wasted. Its energy squandered and resources bungled. It consumes the opportunities of the day in frivolous activities that might leave the day sprinkled here and there with a bit of fun, but fun can't fill the emptiness of a day wasted. It's seen as something for those who are less than serious about life, or for those who haven't really grown up and probably never will. So, some of us don't play around with play because it doesn't play into our conceptualization of life or our commitment to whatever goals we're committed to.

Erring in Balance – "Fooling Around"

Whatever category that we happen to fall into, we all end up 'fooling around' at one time or another. We might do that with a whole bunch of levity, or we might do it with the utmost of seriousness where levity has no place in it at all. We might cautiously approach it in a very conservative manner, or we might rush headlong into it with an unbridled liberality. But we all 'fool around' at one time another. And we all do it differently.

Quite often, 'fooling around' is really undergirded by some objective in the fooling. We're out to achieve something, or make a statement, or reposition ourselves, or bring something to a close, or bring something into play. It might be to make a statement, or not make a statement. It might be to move something along or slow something down. But too often 'fooling around' has an objective that we would be wise to be aware of. Too often there's an ulterior motive that's really driving what we're doing, and too often that ulterior motive is not all that healthy.

And so, our ulterior motives might be related to revenge, where we're out to get back at someone for some perceived offense. Other times it might be related to moving ourselves up in some career or out of some relationship. It might really be about making ourselves feel better because we're not feeling all that good about something, or it might be about making someone else feel worse because we feel that's what they deserve to feel. 'Fooling around' might be about pushing the proverbial envelope because we've become sick and tired of living with integrity and abiding by some moral standard because of the perceived constraints that such living sometimes seems to come with. Maybe we want to spice our lives up a bit and 'play with fire' or 'dance with the devil' as they say to see what all of that's really like.

Too often we equate 'fooling around' as being something that hands us a momentary 'free pass' to explore life in ways that we wouldn't normally explore it. We see it as rather adventurous, and we equate this kind of adventurous behavior as part of living a truly adventurous and robust life. We visualize 'fooling around' as the gate that we need to open up every now and then because if we don't, we'll never really know what's on the other side of that gate. We assume that it's 'walking the line' so that we can better understand where the line is, which is often the justification that we use to figure out just how far we can step over it without stepping into something that we'd prefer not to step into.

And when we start 'fooling around' in these ways, we'll fool ourselves into believing that the choices that we're making are enriching, broadening, enlivening, safe, and profoundly growth-inducing. In reality, they are anything but any of these things. In reality, 'fooling around' foolishly diminishes us, reduces us, robs us blind, strips us bare, erodes the very things that we're trying to build, and eventually destroys us. Fooling around is being the fool. And the danger in 'fooling around' in this manner is that we've fooled ourselves into believing something entirely different.

Refusing to Play the Fool

We can play the fool. And at some time or another we all do. Some more, some less, but we all play the fool at some time. We need to play hard, and we need to have those moments when we 'fool around' in a manner that's immersed in levity and lathered in laughter of the greatest sort. But we need to do so in a manner wisely informed by wisdom, safely shaped by a Godly morality, and unerringly guided around every potential pitfall by a strong sense of ethics.

We need to 'fool around' in a manner that's not pushing any envelope, but in a manner that's pressing us ever-deeper into God and pushing us out into the furthest expanses of who God created us to be. 'Fooling around' is not about some sort of self-proclaimed liberation, rather it's about enjoying the liberty of living in total fullness without being totally destroyed in the living. It's understanding that play is not permission, nor is it license to step over lines because we were just having too much fun. Rather, it's an ingenious creation of God that constantly reminds us that the journey might be arduous, but it is the intricate balance of play and work walking hand-in-hand that ignites those journeys to destinations that we thought to be forever beyond our reach.

When we 'fool around' in this manner, it makes 'fooling around' something of the truly freeing experience that God wants us to fully experience. God wants us to play hard and play long and play with unparalleled exuberance. He designed us to cut loose and 'fool around' in a manner where we're dynamically enriched in the process, and others are enriched right along with us. We want to 'fool around' in a manner than enhances every other aspect of our lives in the playing. God invites you that 'fool around' in a manner that doesn't make a fool out of you but leads you to fullness in every area of your life. And so, embrace wisdom, take hold of a sense of Godly morality, and pull a strong ethic around you and go play. You're most certain to have a total blast.

Chapter Twenty-One
"Good" as the Enemy of the "Best"
Subtly Settling

"So whoever knows the right thing to do and fails to do it, for him it is sin."
-James 4:17 (NIV)

"If you set out to be liked, you would be prepared to compromise on anything at any time, and you would achieve nothing."
- Margaret Thatcher

"That's good enough." How many times have those words come out of our mouths? That phrase seems to have become the rather grating and somewhat pathetic clarion call of a culture that appears to have gone soft and lazy. The idea of this lackluster commitment to the living out of our lives has become so prevalent that we've learned to articulate it in a whole bunch of different ways. The rather robust vernacular that we've created to wave off responsibility and say, "that's good enough" includes such catchy phrases as "that's about as tight as it gets," or "that's within acceptable parameters," or "that'll get us by until Monday," or "that's good enough for government work," or "that's doable," or "that's in the ballpark," or however we say, "that's good enough."

Too often we're choosing to reach up just enough to barely scrape the underside of some pathetically minimal threshold or marginally acceptable norm and call it good. We're deciding to squeak by. Our goal is not the "best," or anything within earshot of it. In fact, many times the whole idea of doing our best doesn't even come close to crossing the frontal lobe of our brain.

Getting It Done Instead of Giving It Our Best

Rather than thinking about how we give our best, we're tediously thinking about how we can give ourselves a break by getting this done as fast as we can get it done in a way that's minimally inconvenient to ourselves. Or the other tact is to postpone "good" by performing an irreverently sloppy patch job out of a less than total commitment that we'll come back to it later, which we typically have no intention of doing. Our goal becomes that which we might barely describe as "good" (if we stretch the definition far enough). And we do this stuff because our desire to get it 'done' perpetually overrides the need to make it 'good' in the doing.

The Evolution of Just Getting By

The marginalizing mentality of just getting by is really nothing new. We seem to be seeing quite a bit more of it today, but it's clearly been a mentality that has plagued mankind throughout mankind's existence. We're always looking to "cut corners," or take a "short-cut," or "short-sheet" whatever we're doing. The whole phenomena of "sliding by" or "skating by" has always been a byword of history.

But there seems to be a dangerous evolutionary turn

these days. We've moved from 'cutting corners' to cutting out work altogether. By all appearances it seems that we're transitioning from taking the 'short-cut' to refusing to get on the path in the first place. It seems that we're doing a whole lot less of the 'short-sheeting' thing and we're 'short-circuiting' anything that we don't like or will demand something of us. And whether we're 'sliding by' or 'skating by,' we're too often saying 'good-bye' to responsibility.

It seems that we want to live a life of privilege. We want the material goods, the ease, the comfort, the bounty, the freedoms, the rights and the privileges. We want the 'good life' however we might define that for ourselves. We want kick back, immerse ourselves in all things pleasurable, breath in the sweet air of ease, all the while generously sipping and savoring all that life has to offer. In short, too often we want what we have not earned. We want pleasure without the pain. We want the wealth without the work. We want to taste life's delicacies without the demands of earning them. We 'want' a lot of things, but it seems that increasingly we 'want' to believe that these are things are not a natural outcome of work, but an automatic part of privilege.

Subsequently, any vague concept of a 'work ethic' seems to have become much less an ethic and much more of a remotely fuzzy idea. It seems that it's no longer a concrete principle that we corporately agree on, that we soundly build our communities and culture on, and unite around in an effort to maximize the quality of our lives and our existence. A work ethic seems to have become a less than appealing idea. Because it's seen as less than appealing, it seems a whole culture is developing that devises ingenious ways to side-step this increasingly antiquated idea. We're constantly working out ways of how not to work. And in doing that, we forfeit doing all the incredible things we could be doing.

What I Need is Simply There

It seems that in the side-stepping a work ethic we're embracing the dangerous notion that others will provide these things for us as a natural course of how things naturally are. There is a rather devious mentality that out there somewhere, some vaguely mysterious person or group of people are working to provide all of this stuff. The belief is that their efforts, absent of my own, are wholly sufficient to maintain this lifestyle that I have not worked for. In the natural evolution of this societal food chain, things just show up without any involvement from us in the showing up. We're sleepily lulled into believing that this is just how it all works. This mentality seems to be gaining acceptance, and in the gaining it is gnawing away at the foundations of our culture.

There seems to be a second twist to this as well. Many of us also seem to have developed this fairy-dust type of magical thinking where things will just be there for us without anyone putting there. Because we can't see the efforts and the work of those who fill the shelves of our stores, or keep the wheels of commerce greased, or who relentlessly ply the seas of a forty-plus hour work week, or those who stand at the ready to defend us or help us they tend to become invisible. And in time, we tend to forget their existence and what they're doing out there to provide us the privilege of having things over here. And so, things are just there because they're there. And because that's the case, we can enjoy them without the guilt of having done nothing to put them there.

Good Verses Best

When this happens, what we are capable of is entirely lost. Our gifts, talents and abilities are sacrificed on the altar of laziness and entitlement. The possibilities that we were created for become improbabilities. The magnificent things that we could have achieved become mangled and lost in the abject futility of living on our laurels. We stand on the end of some perpetual conveyor belt that shovels things in our direction while we simply sit around and wait for them to roll off the end of the belt. The whole of our existence falls to atrophy. Subsequently, we lose who we are, we lose what we could do, and in essence we lose our lives.

At best, whatever our best could have been is lost. Tragically, in time we gradually lose a sense that we could actually do great things, and we forfeit the transformational reality that our best is both achievable and far beyond anything we could imagine with the best of our imaginations. Our best is far better than we think it to be, and because that's the case, our best is able to raise us to heights unimagined and grant us successes that we were certain would have bested us. We forget that we were made to function at our best.

We forget that what our best can actually achieve is not some dreary dream or fabricated fantasy or distant goal so far beyond our reach that it's better not to try and be our best. To be our best is the best thing we can be.

When we surrender to apathy and expect the world to deliver everything to us, we deliver ourselves to a slow death and we sacrifice the best of our potential to the worst of our decisions. Believing that we don't really have to contribute is both a lie and a death-knell. We will gradually waste away, living out a life drown in apathy, choked to a comatose state by mediocrity, and eventually killed without us even knowing that we're dead. This has nothing to do with the best that was intended for us, and it has nothing to do with the best that was built into each of us.

Being Your Best

Being our best is a decision that we make every day. It's a decision of faith, believing that God has called to do our best, and that the best in us and the best of life is achieved when we do consistently do our best. Life is not a journey where we scavenge off the sweaty brows of others or gorge ourselves on the generosity (or obligation) of society. Being our best is realizing that at best, such choices will kill the best within us.

Being our best is asking how can we take ourselves to our own limits in any given situation? It's asking, how do I intentionally leave every situation and every person with more than what they had when I first encountered them? Being our best involves walking away from every situation with less than what we had when we encountered it because we left something behind in the exchange. Being our best asks did we pull out all the stops, and did we press it as far as was humanly possible, and did we walk away with nothing else we could have given? Being our best is realizing that we can never be our best by hoarding. In the wonder of life, we can only be our best by giving and so are we always in the process of giving or preparing to give? In short, being our best is bringing the best of ourselves to the best of others out of a commitment to make their lives the best. Or to put it succinctly, are we being everything that Jesus was to everyone around him?

And so, commit to being your best. Adamantly shun anything that is anything less than that. Realize that you were created to best your own ideas of what your best is. Be your best and in doing so transform yourself and transform those around you in the best way possible.

Chapter Twenty-Two
The Face in the Mirror
The Pain of Having to Face Ourselves

"What a wretched man I am! Who will rescue me from this body that is subject to death?'

- Romans 7:24 (NIV)

"The unexamined life is not worth living."

- Socrates

Do I really want to see myself? Really? Not as I might prefer to see myself in order to have some rickety and ill-placed semblance of peace. Not the image that grants me permission to stay a course that maybe I should stay away from. Not the perception of myself that allows me to side-step guilt, by-pass accountability, and circumvent obligations that I find a bit distasteful. Not the self-that's easy on the eyes of a culture gone blind or fits nicely in a social circle that's spinning in circles. Not the self that the boss is more likely to promote or the person who can more easily fly under the radar of these turbulent times. All of that aside, do I really want to see myself? Really?

We tend to craft an image of ourselves that fits what we'd like to be, but not necessarily what we are. We're quite adept at recognizing what's culturally acceptable so that we can be acceptable to the culture. We know what fits in the tight social circles within which we circulate, and we have some grasp of the latest trends as we see them spread across magazine covers and splashed across our television screens. In no way are we short on examples served up by the culture, and we are perpetually subject to a bevy of obstinate expectations associated with those examples. In artfully and sometimes rather stumbling ways we draw from these various examples and expectations, crafting our image so that we fit whatever they happen to be at the moment.

Confusion in the Shaping

And in the shaping, we incessantly focus on what we're supposed to be, which is perpetually held in some jarring tension against this sense of who we actually are. We frequently sit juxtaposed between an authentic self that frequently doesn't fit into the tightly defined rubrics of a disingenuous culture. Over time, we develop an ever-morphing confusion regarding our identity as this constant tension too often plays itself out on the side of what's expected of us verses who we authentically are.

There is no bridging the gap. No hybrid exists. We are either true to ourselves or we betray ourselves to be true to a culture that's not likely to be true to us. Yet, our attempts to fashion some essential mix leaves us lost, perplexed, and selling our lives out to the bane of compromise.

The battle incessantly incurred by this tension leaves us little time and inadequate energy to explore our core selves, as such an endeavor carried out with diligence will always ask the best of us. The mad chase to be whatever it is that will be accepted (to the greatest degree that it can be accepted) in conjunction with the elusive hunt to obtain whatever it is that allows us to blend in with a world that is itself trying to blend in . . . all of that consumes all of our time. And in the consumption, we are never free enough to ask who it is that we really are.

Maybe We Don't Want to Know

The reality might be that we don't want to know who we are. In part, maybe this incessant pursuit is in reality flight from who we fear we might be. Maybe the person that we attempt to craft is something that we perceive as a bit shinier and slightly more striking in comparison to the person that we actually are. Maybe the image that the world propagates is better. Maybe, just maybe the world knows something that we don't know. Maybe we'd rather be shaped by the world rather than being shaped by histories that are painful, or losses that are devastating, or belief systems that were forced upon us, or dreams that were forced into us.

It might be that we don't like who life has made us to be, so we haplessly gawk at those vogue and savvy examples of what it is to be a vibrant and exuberant person. Maybe society's sales pitch has hooked us, and we find ourselves fawning over airbrushed facsimiles and photo-shopped caricatures. We believe it's more about making ourselves and less about discovering ourselves, as discovering our true selves might be the exact kind of discovery that we never want to discover.

Or just maybe we want a bigger hand in making us

who we've become over and above everything else that has taken license to shape us in whatever way we've been shaped. Maybe we want to call the shots instead of responding to all of the wounds that we carry from all of the many times that others have shot us. It just might be that we're done being some inert lump of clay that all the wrong hands have shaped, and now we want to do the shaping.

But in the end, do we really want to know who we are? And is this fear of knowing in reality a fear of self. Is it a fear of what we might find if we scratch the surface a bit? Is it a throbbing apprehension of what sits down there in those dark places that would forever brutalize us should we bring it to the light? Have our lives been so marked by running 'from' ourselves that running 'to' ourselves is something that we don't even understand how to do? Is our goal to reinvent ourselves away from those dark places rather than rediscover ourselves because what we think we'd discover isn't all that appealing? Or do we assume that an image is something that is crafted rather than something that is cultivated?

The Richness of Running to Self

I would propose that the most potent person that we can become begins with the solitary, yet immensely challenging task of being the person that we are. That may in fact be the most difficult part of this journey that we call life. The greatest 'us' begins with the authentic 'us.' That means that we must be willing to park ourselves wherever we're at, rein in our rather rogue passions, place the press of societal expectations aside, forcefully yet tactfully strip away all the variant facades, and accept whatever we find as our point of departure.

While I tend to run from me, I need to decide to run to me. And in the running I am going to seek out and boldly seize the strengths that I have ignored or altogether abandoned. I will hunt them down, dig them up, brush them off, breath the life back into them that I stole from them, and adamantly refuse to ever abandon them again.

It may well be that I have spent my life incessantly looking for things outside of me that are already within me. It would be entirely prudent to embrace an entirely different tact that involved recognizing these hidden attributes, learning to warmly appreciate them, and then robustly enhancing them in a perpetual cycle of personal growth that we could have hardly imagined as possible.

Where It Begins

First, it begins with intention not bridled by fear. It involves the impetus of possibilities to offset the impotence of impossibilities in order to actually challenge the impossible. It's an intention to grow despite the obstacles that currently lay across our path, as well as press through the obstacles that will arise as a response to our efforts to press forward. It begins by recognizing that the greatest fear is not in what we will find, but in what we will miss if we don't work to find it. It all begins with a passion to grow that will not heed nor be dimmed by the challenges that in and of themselves will bring growth simply by virtue of our choice to engage them.

Second, authentic growth can only begin with an authentic start. That means that we must focus on who we are, which is typically quite different from who we've become. This focus is achieved by brazenly identifying the assorted facades, fearlessly calling them out, audaciously casting them off, and then embracing both the glory and gore of that which lies underneath. It is that glory and gore that is the raw material from which we build a self beyond anything that any collection of facades could hope to fabricate. It's getting down to the raw material, which may be quite raw at times. But it's recognizing that the raw material is both the seedbed and the soil from which God will grow the greatness of who He designed us to be.

Third, we must secure the resources that are above us and adamantly avoid those that are below us. It is a commitment to an upward ascent that is never compromised by a downward mentality. It's the climb that is never not the climb. This means that we refuse anything that generates a lateral move or grants us permission to grow in place, neither of which have anything to do with growth. We must find those people seasoned with wisdom, seize those resources that are unashamedly bold, and be willing to allow those resources to speak into our lives even when their messages are hard and sharp.

The Face in the Mirror

The face in mirror is a great one already, which stands ready to be made greater still. It can be done when we choose to press through fear, tear ourselves down to our authentic self, and intentionally seek out challenging resources to assist in our growth. It's committing to the journey and living for the ride. And when we do, the person that we've shaped ourselves to be will pale in comparison to the person we are now on our way to becoming.

Chapter Twenty-Three
Remodeling or Restoration
Picking Up God's Blueprint

"Do not conform to the pattern of this world but be transformed by the renewing of your mind. Then you will be able to test and approve what God's will is--his good, pleasing and perfect will. ... Then you will learn to know God's will for you, which is good and pleasing and perfect."

- Romans 12:2 (NIV)

"When she transformed into a butterfly, the caterpillars spoke not of her beauty, but of her weirdness. They wanted her to change back into what she always had been. But she had wings."

- Dean Jackson

Jesus never shirks from calling us up and calling us out. He has an uncompromisingly keen and inescapably penetrating way of recognizing life aside from the soiled shades and mediocre tones that mankind has relentlessly painted life in. We have spent thousands of years recklessly hacking away at, and sloppily painting over the creation around us. It seems that it never quite suits us. It appears that there's always some alteration either large or small that we deem to be important or superior to the original design. We have an assorted array of perceived enhancements that we're itching to apply to the world around us, and so we'd better get about the business of altering whatever it is that needs altering.

Renegade Remodeling

It seems that we seldom look at life long enough to appreciate the unmatchable qualities that exist at every turn. With our frequently cavalier determination to remodel it all, we don't want to be bothered with the fact that many times what we're out to remodel is something that's already so immeasurably grand that we could never hope to enhance it in the first place. Neither can we replicate it once we've messed with it. In such situations, at best remodeling becomes irrelevant, and at worst it becomes irreverent. With saw, hammer, power tools and paint in hand, we don't like hearing that. We unthinkingly step up and we commence with some sort of rogue remodeling of whatever's around us without ever really taking the time to see what we're remodeling before we begin chopping it up. And because we do, we seem to seldom take the wiser course of careful observation that's most often followed by thoughtful preservative instead of thoughtless devastation.

An Infinite Blueprint

It would be remiss not to point out that mankind has made some great, and at times rather stunning contributions to this thing called 'life' that we're all living. There is within each of us some scant blueprint of infinite design that on occasion we refer to, and in the referring we marvel at the unfathomable complexity and intricate beauty that's laid out in that absolutely stunning blueprint. When we actually refer to God's blueprint, we gladly work in fascinated conjunction with it, suddenly realizing that any other action outside of that blueprint is foolhardiness and lunacy of the worst sort. When we work in cooperation with God's blueprint, seemingly impossible feats are actually achieved. Things beyond our comprehension are repeatedly accomplished. Yet far too often we don't refer to the blueprint at all. And in some instances when we actually do, we often take artistic license with it and hastily edit it to our own likings. And every time we do that, something dies.

Remodeling from Bad Blueprints

We've certainly done our own bit of remodeling with the life that we've been granted, and it takes little more than a quick glance around at the state of things to realize that we've made quite a mess of it. Our 'additions' to life have more often than not turned out to be gross 'deletions.' Our attempts to modify life in some capacity has at times found us crucifying it instead. In building it up, we've often torn it down. And in building it out, we've too often blown it out instead. Many of our efforts to intentionally craft and subsequently force our limited vision on life has more often than not resulted in some degree of cataclysm or schism or division or any number of other things that aren't all that savory. And those efforts ended up playing themselves out quite a distance from what we had originally envisioned because we put God's blueprint aside in lieu of our own.

Remodeling seems to be in our blood. It seems that we're built to tear down and build up. We have this relentless need to improve upon whatever we're improving upon. There's always the next possibility, a shining array of other alternatives, a bucket full of untouched options that all glisten brightly, each of them screaming for our attention all at the same time. There's always the next thing, the next step, the next trend, the next phase, the next addition, and the next deletion that makes way for the next addition after that. And it's not that remodeling is bad. In fact, we ourselves seem to be designed for it. It's simply that remodeling while blithely casting aside God's blueprint in the remodeling will always leave us blue in ways that no amount of remodeling can ever fix.

The Ultimate Restoration Specialist

Jesus was and is the greatest restoration specialist of all time. He possesses the sole and solitary advantage of having created all of life in the first place. The blueprint for all of life was drawn up from the infinite pallet of His infinitely creative genius, and it was painted on a canvas that stretches infinitely beyond the place where the most distant galaxy ends. God created an existence that the existence itself can only marginally understand, much less replicate. God fashioned a created order that exceled that very order itself. He designed creation beyond creation itself so that wonder would never find a place where it would be forced to pull up and cease to exist because there was nothing left to wonder at. God designed creation with enough room that there would always be room to marvel and ample space to wonder. And all of that is ingeniously marvelous and terribly wonderful.

The Cost of Our Remodeling for Us

But it seems that we've made a wonderful mess of it in so many ways. And in the making of this tangled and knotted mess of ours, we've made a real mess of ourselves as well. It would be advisable to realize that we will eventually become whatever it is that we've created. And too often what we've created is a massive mess. Subsequently, we've diminished ourselves, demoralized ourselves, displaced ourselves, and in doing so we've solidly placed ourselves on a certain path of certain destruction. In far too many situations, our tedious remodeling has not served us or the creation that we've been busy remodeling because we threw out God's blueprint in favor of our own.

Inevitably, we've settled for less. We have settled for a world of our own shaping that is shaping up to be in terrible shape. We have subjugated ourselves to our own finite and pathetically selfish designs, and as a consequence we have left ourselves far, far less than God's original blueprint intended us to be. We are, in too many ways, a painfully marred and dauntingly cheapened shadow of something that was designed to be much more robust, exceedingly more expansive, and whole lot more of everything than what we've turned out to be. Too many times, the very pride that drives our remodeling keeps us from humbly coming before God, honestly acknowledging the incredible mess that we've made, letting go of our blueprints, and allowing Him to restore what we've remodeled.

Jesus Came to Restore Our Remodeling

Coming to Him is exactly what God desires that we

to do. Jesus says, "I have come that they may have life, and have it to the full." Or to put it another way, Jesus came to restore our remodeling. What it's really all about is squarely centered on the fact that He came to restore the original intent of all of this. Jesus stands ready to restore our remodeling, which suggests that our remodeling must have something really wrong with it. If God Himself has to undo what we have done, we might be wise to consider what we've done so we don't do any more of it.

But the key is not just the restoration of life as some sort of nice idea, or a quick touch up of the damage that we've done. It's not about something cheaply cosmetic, or some half-hearted effort that makes things a bit more presentable. Jesus says that He came to give us "life to the full." Life to the maximum. Life to the very edges of life. Life that includes everything that we can see, and life that doesn't leave out a single thin shard of the far greater portion that we can't even begin to see. To give us life without leaving out any of life in the giving. To give us life with no-holds barred, and without any hint of skimping in the giving. Life that is full and running over. "Life to the full." A life that our remodeling has in many instances actually worked against. And because we've worked against it, we've become accustomed to the pathetically bottom-feeding standards and life-sucking paradigms that leave us weak, anemic and bled of life. And so, "life to the full" is entirely alien to us because we've worked hard to undo it and in the undoing we are undone.

Remodeling or Restoration?

So what will we do? Will we continue on with our remodeling as notoriously ineffectual and damaging as that has apparently been? Will we continue to toddle on with tools in hand, bumping from one thing to another and hacking away at whatever we're bumping into as a means of remodeling what we bump into? Are we going to live a lifestyle that is an attempt to remodel everything to suit our lifestyle, and our biases, and our prejudices? Or are we going to put down our saws, lay down our hammers, turn off our power tools, lay aside all of the agendas that drive all of those tools, and are we going to pick up God's blueprint instead?

Jesus said that He "came to give us life, and life to the full." No blueprint that we can ever fashion will ever do that. No scheme, no strategy, no ploy, and no plan despite how ingeniously constructed and tediously mapped out can ever do what Jesus wants to do for us. And so, at what point will we stop our rampant remodeling, pick up God's blueprint and let Him restore us? The complete blueprint is available to you right now in a single book called the Bible. You may want to pick up a copy and start studying the most phenomenal blueprint ever written.

Chapter Twenty-Four
I Believe
What I Want to Believe

"Immediately the boy's father exclaimed, 'I do believe; help me overcome my unbelief!'"

- Mark 9:24 (NIV)

"You ought to discover some principle, you ought to have some great faith that grips you so much that you will never give it up. Somehow you go on and say, 'I know that the God that I worship is able to deliver me, but if not, I'm going on anyhow, I'm going to stand up for it anyway.'"

- Martin Luther King Jr.

The Need to Believe

We always have, and we always will have the intrinsic need to believe in something. Life is a journey whose demands will always exceed whatever personal assets we might possess in an attempt to meet those demands. Life always has and life always will require more of me than I have within myself to give it. All of my accumulated resources meticulously gathered and shrewdly coordinated in the most strategic manner possible will always fall achingly short of meeting even the most primitive and pared down demands of living life. And because that's the case, I've got no alternative but to extend myself outside of myself and believe in things that are bigger than me. I not only need to believe, I want to believe.

I want to believe, especially in a world that seems to be falling apart in places that I never believed it would fall apart. In the midst of all of the unnerving unraveling that I am helpless to stop, there are things I'd like to believe to calm my heart and steady my soul. There's some sustaining and comforting beliefs that I doggedly want to hold onto that provide me a sense of desperately needed peace in the tumultuous storms that seem to be roaring across the landscape of our culture. I want to believe.

Yet, peace is not enough. To believe in something that can bring me peace, but whose power and reach ends at peace is simply not enough. I need more than that. I need something that can do more than just weather the storms of life and bring me out on the other side with as few bruises as possible. I want to believe in things that have relentlessly stood the test of time, every time, throughout all of time. I want to believe in things that won't fall to the abject recklessness of our times, this time or any time. But far more than that, I want to believe in things that can handily wrestle any storm into full submission. And I want to dare to believe in things that are so pristinely confident and courageously authentic that they could keep the next storm from ever daring to roll across the landscape of our culture again if we all simply chose to believe in those things. I want to believe.

I want to believe in things that have the breathtaking power and the unobstructed reach to reconstruct and reclaim whatever's left when the storm is over. I want to believe that storms are part of life and that they come into the sinful and fallen world that we live in as a natural part of our fallen existence. But far beyond that, I want to believe in things powerful enough and audacious enough to transform the wreckage of the storm right in the middle of the very storm itself. I want to believe in things that can reconstruct and reclaim in a manner that handily resurrects implausible beauty out of what seems to be unredeemable carnage. I want to believe that no storm ever conceived can come close to having the force or the power to dislodge or destroy the things that I believe in. I want to believe in believing because if I can't believe in something, what do I have?

What I'd Like to Believe

I Want to Believe That Mankind is Inherently Good

In the storms, I'd like to believe that mankind is inherently good. I want to believe that even though mankind can act in gruesome ways that push the edge of evil out to appalling places and reign destruction in ways previously unfathomable, that even then there is still some thread of something good weaving itself undaunted through the core of our core. I want to believe that we're lost, that we're drowning in greed and selfishness, and that we've taken to treacherous paths that descend to gaping depths of great atrocity. But I want to believe that those things don't define us. Despite our frequently heinous behaviors, I want to believe that we're better than that because I want to believe that there is no point that we could ever reach from which we cannot be redeemed. I want to believe that mankind is inherently good despite all the apparently inherent evil that would scream otherwise. I want to believe that there is enough good in all of us to be marvelously good if we're daring enough to ruthlessly rid ourselves of everything that keeps us from being marvelous. I want to believe this.

I Want to Believe That a Single Voice for Good is Never Too Small

I want to believe that a single voice for good has a vibrant tenor, a wholly unsullied tone, a dynamically firm volume, and a magnetic quality about it that it will always be heard above, and around, and beyond any chorus of evil despite how loud it might be. I want to believe that voices for good always have an undeniable and unapproachable genuineness about them that renders all fraudulent voices completely exposed and entirely drown out. Too often it seems that a single voice for good is quickly submerged under the surging tsunami other voices which are anything but good. Evil and treachery seem to be boisterous and arrogant, bellowing with an unashamed narcissistic quality that aims to quash any voice with even the remotest hint of good in it. I want to believe that a voice for good will incessantly rise above the most bellicose volume that evil can produce, and that it will always render evil frustrated in its inability to drown out a single voice for good. I want to believe that single voice can do exactly that. I want to believe this.

I Want to Believe That Good is Eternal and Evil is Temporal

I want to believe that evil is not part of what this was originally all about. I want to believe that evil was not an original component of creation as it was sketched out on the original drawing board innumerable eons ago. I want to believe that evil is an infestation that wormed its way into our existence and as such can be eradicated because it is an infestation, and only an infestation. I want to believe that it is a cancerous plague that has no claim of originality in the original design. I want to believe that evil is a temporary foe that lives on a short leash of time, and that every battle finds that leash shortened one more constricting link. I want to believe that good will ultimately exterminate evil in a manner so complete that every battle will be forever laid to rest, and that the memory of those battles will likewise be laid to rest, and that good itself will be able to securely rest for the rest of eternity. I want to believe this.

I Want to Believe That God Uses Evil to Advance Good

I want to believe that God will not be thwarted by the greatest exploits that evil can conjure up. I want to believe that evil will always find itself obliterated by its own evil as God seizes it, shapes it into invincible good, and then sends it hurtling right back into the heart of the very evil from which it came. I want to believe that the greater the treachery and the more profound the wickedness, the more substance God has to mold good from. That in the hands of God, everything vile is the raw material from which He can forge something astonishingly marvelous. And that everything foul provides the very flames within which these good and great things are forged. I want to believe that in the firing, that which God has forged becomes something so hardened that the most intense fires of evil itself cannot even remotely singe it. I want to believe that as evil escalates in intensity, it only creates a greater abundance of raw material from which good is forged, fired, and fired against evil. I want to believe this.

I Want to Believe that Believing is Not Childish

Believing is not childish nor is it naïve. It's not some escapist refuge where the weak flee in the face of the daunting cultural upheavals that now beset our culture and hound those of us who believe. Believing will make us a ready target for those who don't believe, and it will draw skeptics and naysayers to us as bees to honey. Believing means that we invest in what we can't see, we hand ourselves over to that which we can't control, and we cast our lot with the eternal verses the less demanding demands of the temporal. Belief is not for the frail or faint-hearted as belief will demand belief of us, which is a demand far beyond most anything else in our lives. And because of those realities, I want to believe.

Believing is being courageous enough to relentlessly hold onto the truth even when the derogatory actions of everything around us would attempt to entirely discredit the truth, smear the truth, and completely supplant it with falsehoods dressed in the look-a-like garments of truth. By making the uncompromising commitment to stand on our beliefs, we declare that the truth on which we have chosen to stand is nothing of unreliable myth or childish fantasy. And that will certainly draw the ire of many. Believing is standing on the truth even when everything else around us has fallen into cinders and ash, and the truth on which we're precariously standing continues to be pounded by everything that hates the very truth that we're standing on. And for all of those reasons, I want to believe.

I Want to Believe in God

Believing is costly. Believing is sacrificial. Believing is what the majority of the world doesn't have the guts to do, but it is the only thing to do. I want to believe this. And of all the things that I want to believe, I want to believe in God above and beyond all of them. To believe in God in the face of everything that would tell us not to believe is the highest calling of mankind, and the greatest feat of our existence. To believe in God is to extend ourselves beyond our finite existence and cast our belief out into the unfathomable reaches of the infinite. To believe in God is to stake our lives on something that the world declares as a mistake. But to believe in God is to wager everything on the person who created everything, and no mistake could ever arise out of that. Without God, I don't have the capacity to believe in anything else anyway as everything emerges from Him. And so, I want to believe in God, I want to believe in every one of His promises, and I want to believe in all of the things that He allows me to believe in. I want to believe. With all my heart I want to believe. And I want you to believe as well.

Chapter Twenty-Five
The Known as Keys to the Unknown
Boldly Stepping Forward

"Then the LORD said to him, 'What is that in your hand?' 'A staff,' he replied."
- Exodus 4:2 (NIV)

"A man is original when he speaks the truth that has always been known to all good men."
- Patrick Kavanagh

What lies ahead of us is shrouded in the milky fog of mystery and the confounding muse of speculation that such mystery provokes. What lies behind us might tempt us to mystery and speculation, but it will only do so in regard to making sense of what lies behind us. What lies back there is only unknown in that we have yet to figure it out. But as we do, it remains a steady reference as it is history written. Therefore, it is embedded in the immovable place that we call history.

And in this thing called 'time' and in this journey that we call 'life,' we are firmly and forever sandwiched between the known and the unknown, between the past and the present. We live on the departing edge of that which is known but past, and we stand on the teetering precipice of that which is unknown and certain to come in whatever manner it comes. The future sweeps in to become the present, and in no time at all it is swept out to become the history that we've shaped it to be. And in this incessant cavalcade of time flowing, we stand at the exact point where the future becomes the past.

What we know, we know forever. But what we know at this moment is not the 'forever' of our knowledge. It is what we know at the moment, and what we know at the moment prepares us for what we are yet to know in the future. Life is not stagnant, and neither is the knowledge that we need to navigate it. We exist in this tension between what we already know and that which we don't know, for both are essential to an advancing existence. It's the fluid dance of that which we know and that which we don't that allows us to celebrate the past (or heal from it) while fully embarking upon our journey into an advancing future.

While what we know is clear (or possibly not so clear), what we don't know is neither. In fact, we probably don't know what it is that we don't know. It lies ahead of us, either a mere step away or possibly many years away (whatever the case might be). But we cannot live simply on what we know, for that builds walls and erects barriers that stifle our existence, suffocate our vision, and bring an end to our existence long before death shows up to do that. There is the 'yesterday' of our memory and the 'tomorrow' of our imagination. Both brought together allows us to advance in life in ways that we hadn't thought possible.

There must be the unknown, for without it our life comes to a dreaded halt right where we stand. The known serves the present, while the mysterious configuration of both of the known and the unknown are the essential ingredients of any future. To fear the unknown and press it aside is to assume that the future will not demand something of us that we don't know. It is to believe that the future can be built solely on the past without the creativity, innovation and freshness that something new will always demand out of something old.

Living Between the Known and Unknown

Living within the opposing poles of this conflicting conundrum wherein the past is known with all the comforts and angst of knowing, and the future is unknown with all the anxiety that such mystery spawns, we often become stalled. What is known might be painful in a manner that breeches human tolerance or devastating in a manner that drives us to the ghastly abyss of hopelessness. It might scream at us with some high-pitched insanity, or it may whisper in a manner that is quiet, but maddeningly incessant. Yet it is known, which renders it predictable and safe because it's cast and petrified in the permanence of history past. It will never be more than what it is because it is forever bound to what it was.

The future has no such permanence. The future will only become petrified when it becomes a present reality, and after having done so it rolls off into the past to bc permanently cast in the annuals of an unchangeable history. It becomes permanent not 'when' the footprints are made. It becomes permanent 'once' they are made. The future is a thick mist, sometimes moving aside just enough to tease us with a slight glimpse of what lays in wait for us. As quickly as it moved aside it rolls back in, wrapping a veil of mystery around the mystery that is the future. Something's out there, but we're not quite certain exactly what that is, or where it is.

Yet, we are left with the vexing reality that once we have impounded what was once unknown in an immovable past, the next unknown immediately steps up to us. To live is to celebrate what is known but to simultaneously embrace the unknown, for this is the essential part of the coming-and-going in life. And so, it is always the case that the past is irreparably land-locked, and the future has yet to land. And here we are, living out our lives on the precariously thin line which separates the two.

Forever Stalled

Frequently, we prefer neither of the two options which leaves us abjectly stranded in our disappointment of life. The known of our past holds both good, bad and all the assorted variations in-between, but it is locked tight and affords us nothing other than what it is. We are stuck with what has passed. What has passed might be good, or it might be bad, or it might be neither. It could hold the warmest of moments or the darkest of horrors. But in whatever places it falls, we can't rewrite it, improve upon it, modify it, or take an eraser (of whatever kind that might be) and make it different. It's set in stone that is either warm and comforting, cold and barren, or somewhere in-between.

To the contrary, the unknown of the future offers us unimagined possibilities and wide-open venues. It's not bound by anything other than our fears or stunted imaginations. It's filled with a thousand horizons and an equal number of possibilities. However, it is plagued with risk and inundated with uncertainty. It is the platform upon which we can do better, be better, and go farther. It can't rewrite the past, but it can write something entirely different than the past. It can't change the carnage that lays strewn across the road of our history, but it can pave new roads that know nothing of carnage. The future can be the place where we can prove that we are not the stuff of our past, and that we are made of better 'stuff' than our past would suggest.

Yet, as we noted the future is not certain. We don't know where the pitfalls are or how close to the edge of any cliff we might be. We may know the friends that will walk out there with us, but we may not know the enemies that have laid their many traps in advance of our arrival. We're not entirely certain what the demands will be or when they'll show up. We're not certain that it won't mimic our past in manner that convinces us that our past will be our forever future. We don't know if the future will move fast or if it will slog along. It may be gracious to us or it may be anything but gracious. The future is not certain, and therein lies the risk.

Standing in the In-Between

And so, we stand moribund on this thin line. We are standing in-between what was and what will be. The known and the unknown. The familiar and the unfamiliar. That which is concluded, and that which is yet to begin to move toward that end. We incessantly vacillate between what's behind us and what's before us depending on the current barometer of our courage and the ambivalent nature of our vision. Sometimes we step back. In our braver moments, we step forward. And in moments of accelerating panic and duress, we freeze in place. And in the end, we often move very little (if at all).

The Known as the Handbook for the Unknown

We have naively forgotten that the unknown is not an option. Whether we wish it or not, life is constantly propelling us into the milky mystery of the future. Any sense that we have an option as to such a journey is something of a fictional myth and foolish notion. To not go forward is to go backward.

Since the journey into the unknown is indisputably non-negotiable, we would be wise to recognize that the known is the perfect handbook and flawlessly crafted tool that we have to effectively engage the unknown. Do we not realize that the known is the very thing that assists us in navigating the unknown? Should we fear the unknown or should we realize that everything that we know has been given to us to navigate that which we do not. It's not about fearing what we don't know. It's about realizing that we've been granted the information, the insights, and the experiences that help us to not only decipher the unknown, but to maximize it for our growth and advancement. As God said to Abraham, "Go from your country, your people and your father's household to the land I will show you" (Genesis 12:1 (NIV). In the same manner, we can and should go.

Life is not about a choice between the known and unknown, between where we are and where we're not. Rather, it's about recognizing that the resources birthed and spun from the 'known' are the perfect resources to engage, embrace and seize the 'unknown.' There is a nearly magical confluence where one permits the embrace of the other. It's the lessons drawn from what is known that are the very keys to the tumblers of the unknown. Therefore, we need not dance on the precarious line between the two. Rather, we reach backward into the known to seize the perfectly crafted resources to move forward into the unknown. And it is here, in embracing this priceless reality that we can run into the milky fog of the future with confidence instead of cowardice, fortitude instead of fear, and a heart ceaselessly emboldened by hope instead of incessantly undercut by hesitation. It is here that we live.

Chapter Twenty-Six
The End
The Idea That I Could Be

He is not the God of the dead, but of the living, for to him all are alive."

- Luke 20:38

"End? No, the journey doesn't end here. Death is just another path. One that we all must take."

- J.R.R. Tolkien, The Return of the King

"The End." There's something definitively final about those two simple words. Those two, three letter words appear on the screen when the last words of the actors have fallen into an irretrievable silence and the screen has been swept barren of images. They pen an irrefutable and final 'period' on the last page of novels beyond which sentences and syntax utterly cease to exist. These two simple words bring down the final curtain at the end of every play with everything behind the curtain now entirely exhausted and utterly spent in the performance. They are the statement that something has concluded in an irrevocably conclusive manner. "The End."

"The End" indicates that there is no more. Nothing. That something that we enjoyed, or found ourselves swept up in, or something that lifted us in ways that we are rarely lifted is over. A moment that should be part of our lives for the whole of our lives won't be a part of our lives. Something was given and then taken. We sipped something sweet and then we were told that there was only a bit of it to be sipped. It was the great 'bait-and-switch' that teased our imagination and ignited our soul only to be snatched away. Dispirited and forlorn, we would prefer that we had not been given anything at all, rather than to taste something so marvelous and then have it vanish. "The End" just doesn't seem right nor does it appear to be in keeping with what we should have been able to keep.

The Incomprehensible Nature of "The End"

The implication is that something is over. But far more than over, these words imply that something has run the full length of its course and that no other course lies beyond it. The words "The End" suggest that the story has been told to outright completion and that not a single line or scant syllable is left to the tale to tell at some future time. "The End" seems to indicate that whatever has transpired has completely rolled over into lifeless annals of history without any ability on our part to reach out and resuscitate it, leaving nothing in our hands but a shadowy memory of what no longer is. And more despairingly, it all leaves us without any sense that whatever has ended will somehow show up on the horizon of the future to be enjoyed yet again. "The End."

It identifies a definitive end beyond which some larger story, or a fuller appreciation of the story already told, or a sequel of some sort, or even a brief space within which to savor what just transpired exists for the savoring. There's something terribly uncomfortable when we hear the words "The End." They say something that just couldn't be. Something that doesn't match the nature of what we've experienced. We can't envision a point beyond which nothing exists. We have difficulty drawing some line beyond which there is a vast nothingness. There is always the next thing, the next opportunity, the next place within which something is going to happen. There is always the 'next.'

The End?

Despite the finality of it all, we have this terribly tenacious proclivity to fight against the notion that an end is an absolute end. There seems to be such a ruthless totality about it all. Something within us adamantly objects to the finality of an end; something that senses that life is somehow far too grand and immensely too resilient to ever be held captive to endings of any kind despite the magnitude or ferocity of them. There is some possibly primal or likely spiritual sense that shouts that life is far too magnificent to have even the minutest part of it irreparably shut down with such an abrupt finality. It is nearly inconceivable to step up to the line where something expired and to see nothing but 'nothing' beyond the line.

Quite to the contrary, we are swept up in limitless possibilities that infuse endings with the stuff that birth beginnings. We have that unflinching sense that something else always lies out beyond whatever it is that has transpired, copiously prepared and wholly readied to step in in some nearly anointed fashion. We see life as an unrelenting progression rather than a blunted termination. Things give way to other things which in turn give way to yet other things in some undefeatable cycle that stretches eons beyond our imaginations and reaches far beyond the span of our years. In the deep habitations of our souls, there is no "The End."

Life as Cyclic

We live in a world intricately woven of cycles of the most innumerable and improbable sort. Cycles are the persistently consistent story of our lives that weave a circular story that moves forward to new horizons held in the familiarity borne of cycles. Whether it's the titanic cycle of the seasons that sweep the entire globe, or the mitosis of a single cell, everything moves in cycles. Sunrise to sunset. The mass migration of animals forging southward only to trek northward again when spring rubs the land warm. Everything moves from what it is, to what it will be.

Cycles are cycles because they don't end. They perpetuate a freshness, a newness, a rolling on of life that is embedded in the DNA of cycles. Death itself is a cycle, preparing for and enriching that which is to come after it. Life does not move to an end. It moves to the next thing. If we perceive an end as truly as end, it's because we do not have the vision to see the thing that's taking root just underneath the surface of that which has ended.

God's genius is found in the fact that He authored a creation that is adamant in perpetuating itself even in the harshest and most foreboding of situations. Life will overrun every ending with a beginning. No end will ever stand as an end. No end is so powerful that it can stop a beginning. Ever. Beginnings are incessant and ruthless if need be, for life does not stop.

The Character of the Creator

Anything created meticulously and quite ingeniously mirrors even the most subtle attributes of that which created it. The throbbing heart and most intimate soul of anything that has ever been created was intimately shaped by the hands of some creator that birthed it. And in the birthing, every stroke of every creator's hand was dictated by the nature of their heart and the character of their soul.

Is God's character itself embedded in that which He created? How could it not be? And is the force of His power and the infinite nature of His being woven into every living thing? Is that not obvious? Did He call everything into existence in a manner that it could never be called out of existence? Is God the single entity that can create in a manner that what He creates can never be uncreated? Is His stamp one whose impression will never fade, that will never been replaced, that will never be improved upon, and can never be replicated?

Can that which is eternal do anything less than create that which is eternal? Is it possible to create less than Who and What the Creator is? For I find it utterly improbable that God would be anything less than what He is, and that He would not create anything less as well. In fact, is He the sole creator with any other supposed creator only building on what He created? And if that is the case, how can there be an end to anything?

An End as Inconceivable

Therefore, could it be that the relentlessness of the world around us, bolstered by the passionate hunger to survive even in the face of the most heinous and potent threats mirrors the heart of that which spun all of creation into existence? Is it possible that this insistence to press on and overcome is the manifestation of that bit of God that resides within us? Could it be that the inability to embrace the absolute finality of an end simply rests in the fact that there is no end to that which created all that there is?

And if that is indeed the case, then the purposed defense of hope and the sterling promise of a future stand without interruption or threat. If that is the case, the horizon will always be filled with droves of that which will fill, heal and restore the places and spaces left by that which has departed. If that is the case, there is no place where hope is not, where failure is the final word, and where our choices forever lock us into the consequences of those choices.

That is the vitalizing message of this Creator of ours as it is woven in and through all things. And that message means that "The End" is nothing more and nothing less than a beginning infused with great promise and fresh start laced with irrepressible hope.

Chapter Twenty-Seven
The Cross
What It Says and What We Can't

"Salvation is found in no one else, for there is no other name under heaven given to mankind by which we must be saved."

- Acts 4:12 (NIV)

"Salvation cannot be bought with the currency of obedience; it is purchased by the blood of the Son of God. Thinking that we can trade our good works for salvation is like buying a plane ticket and then supposing we own the airline. Or thinking that after paying rent for our home, we now hold title to the entire planet earth."

- Dieter F. Uchtdorf

There is that exhilaratingly incessant drive within us, that unidentified but entirely electrifying spark, that rogue passion that is part of us but whose larger part is so expansive that it seems not to be part of us at all. There are feelings that completely defy our capacity to create, but not our ability to feel. There is a seemingly ludicrous hope that will not die even though the brutal logic of our circumstances has repeatedly left it for dead more times than we can remember.

There is an ornery and wildly stubborn belief that something greater stands above that which is strangling us even though we can't see that 'something greater.'

There is a mysteriously visionary sense that 'what is' exists only to turn into 'what will be,' even though at that very moment 'what will be' is entirely out of our line of sight.

There is that dogged 'will to live;' a will that finds itself remaining astonishingly relentless even when utterly surrounded by the advancing specter of death. There is that obstinate 'drive to achieve;' a nobly stubborn standard that declares that simply running to the edges of ourselves is not enough until we have deliberately run over those edges and then run out so far from them that we can't even see them anymore. There is that fixed 'passion,' where we are driven by a pioneering angst that demands that we let our imaginations roam and find wings to fly in the roaming.

And if we were to trace all of these marvelous and aptly mysterious things back to some point of origin within us, at most times and at most points the line seems to move outside of us. Indeed, all of our accumulated assets and the sum total of our resources all neatly tallied do not seem to reveal sufficient properties to suggest that we are the source of our own attributes or the author of our own passions. In short, we are more than our ability to create.

What the Cross Says
We Are Not Enough

The cross says that we have great capacity, but limited ability to use that capacity. It says that inherently woven within us are assets so phenomenal that we have become caught up in the utter magnitude of them, and in being caught up we have become duped by the power of them. We have come to believe that we are wholly independent, and in that independence, we are wholly unstoppable. We have come to believe in our own adequacy which in fact has bred our inadequacy.

Yet, despite the wondrous nature of our gifting and abilities, the world around us does not in any way remotely reflect those abilities. We live in a world where 29,000 children die every day, which is enough to fill up an average football stadium every three days. There are 1.56 million homeless people in the United States, which means 1 out of every 204 Americans will seek refuge in a shelter or sleep on the street tonight. Roughly 437,000 people are murdered worldwide every year, which is equal to the entire population of Omaha, Nebraska. And while we could go on to list an endless array of innumerable statistics that outline the dark decay of mankind, what we see in our world does not even vaguely reflect the incredible capabilities we possess.

In the face of such discouraging realities, we fabricate solutions of the most creative but inadequate sort. We tediously construct philosophies that promise astounding solutions that render our problems forever vanquished. We formulate medical remedies purporting to perform a host of nearly miraculous healings where we best sickness, crush illness, and push death's timeline ever further out into some feared horizon. We legislate until our pens run dry and our paper runs out. We espouse questionable rights believing that if we throw off the encumbrances of ethics and rip away the chafing constraints of morals, we will have liberated ourselves to some ill-defined euphoric utopia.

We raise up plastic heroes that play the part but rarely are the part. And these supposed heroes spout platitudes that have no depth, possess no bearings, and lack anything substantial enough to stand on. Yet, the masses fall for the thin ideologies and the subsequently the culture falls because of them. The voices are many, and we give too many of them a voice.

But in the end, children continue to die, individuals still sleep on America's streets, and people around the globe continue to be murdered. And if we're truly paying attention to these things, we will quickly realize that we are not enough.

What the Cross Says
Without God We Are Not Enough

The cross is a response to mankind expending all of its accumulated assets, exhausting every resource at its disposal, working every angle possible, tediously editing history, authoring truth to its own liking, and despite such a gloriously misdirected effort, hitting the end of ourselves and hitting that end hard. We have tweaked, twisted, contorted and constricted the things around us in some god-like fashion as a means of solving the problems that sweep through our lives, our communities and our culture. We expend the best of our lives and the sum total of our energies crafting temporal solutions to eternal problems. Yet, children continue to die, individuals still sleep on America's streets, and people around the globe continue to be murdered because without God we are not enough.

The cross is a marvelous affirmation of the genius of our design, but it is likewise the blunt acknowledgement that left to its own devices, the genius of our design will result in the destruction of our lives. Greatness untethered from God results in calamity unrestrained by men. And if that is somehow not enough, the cross is saying that not only will we fall distressingly short of achieving our potential when separated from God, it is saying in no uncertain terms that that potential will be turned to the destruction of itself and ultimately to the destruction of us.

The cross is God's offer of redemption. It's the solution to the limits of our limitations, but it's also the solution to the world's pain. It's the invitation of God for us to unite the depth of our humanity with the eternal nature of His being from which that humanity was birthed. It is the invitation to everything that we could want and all that we need.

We Cannot Redeem Ourselves but the Cross Can

The cross is God's redemptive act whereby He stepped in to save us from the calamity of ourselves so that we can finally step out into the fullness of ourselves. Whether we like it or not, it is saying that the beginnings that we believe we so ingeniously craft are only endings postponed, and that any authentic beginning is something only God can create. The cross holds out the simple truth that the majesty of God generously woven within us will be left to utter rot if we rebelliously force God out of us. And therefore, the cross is the redemption that we cannot deliver, handed to us so that we might live the lives that we could not imagine.

The cross is the boldest and most generous invitation to liberation ever extended. And that invitation invites us to be unleashed from our own disastrous ending so that we might live lives that are gloriously unending. The cross delivers everything that we are finally unleashed and astonishingly freed to be.

When we finally shake ourselves free from the fact that we've been duped by our own sense of inflated grandiosity, and when we surrender to God's liberation, children will live, individuals will sleep in safety, and people around the globe will live out of fullness of their days. And before we dare pass on such an astounding invitation, it would behoove to understand that none of us will ever receive any invitation, despite how grand, that can do all of that.

Chapter Twenty-Eight
Backwards
The Grand Reversal of God

"He is risen."
- Matthew 28:6 (NIV)

"Miracles are not in contradiction to nature. They are only in contradiction with what we know of nature."
- Saint Augustine

Being Backwards

I am backwards. I don't think I'm backwards. I wouldn't necessarily see myself as backwards. I certainly wouldn't suggest that I live my life that way, although I might do a few things every now and then that look a bit backwards. But I am backwards. In fact, I've become so accustomed to living backwards that I've completely confused backwards with forwards. The fact of the matter is most of the culture is doing the same exact thing that I'm doing. No, I wouldn't I tell you that I'm backwards; but I'm backwards.

And the oddity of it all is that I actually see backwards as forwards. From where I'm sitting it doesn't look backwards at all. I can look at my life from a bunch of different angles, and it doesn't look backwards. However, in terms of how I conceptualize the realities of life as held against the limitations that I perceive myself as having, I'm backwards.

Why I'm Backwards

I'm backwards because I have tediously assessed the realities of the existence within which I am forced to operate, and I have concurrently determined the permanently fixed limitations that define my humanity as I live within that existence. And based on the conclusions I have drawn in these two areas, I have done a rather splendid job of setting the parameters for my existence by configuring (to the best of my ability) what's possible and what's not.

In the end, this determination that I have made regarding that which is 'possible' verses that which is 'impossible' is markedly canted toward the 'impossible', leaving me facing a life bereft of everything except a handful of the most limited 'possibilities'. Worse yet, this determination has come to comprehensively define all of life as I know it, leaving me nothing bigger than myself. I have categorized the whole of life as falling within the limits that limit me, assuming these are limits for everything that exists, or ever will exist, or ever could exist. And in that sense, I have dramatically drawn down life into some minute rubric that's but the slightest fraction of what life really is. Indeed, I am backwards.

God's Reversal

We reject God because He is not backwards…at all. He comes to us asking us to move forward, which we, by virtue of our shallow determinations about how life works, see as backwards. And we stand there wondering why we would be asked to do something so utterly preposterous as moving backwards. In fact, what God calls forward we call impossible, or improbable, or ridiculous, or naïve, or fanciful, or ignorant, or any number of other explanations that really do more to explain how backwards we really are.

God calls us to move mountains when we diligently work to figure ways around them. He asks us to pray for the impossible when we don't even pray for the possible. He asks us to believe that He will supply all of our needs, when we live out our lives chasing all of the things that we want. He tells us to love our neighbor while we're working to avoid contact with most of them. He tells us to store up treasures in heaven while we incessantly shop the internet. Either God is backwards, or we are.

Reversals

History is littered with God's reversals. Leprosy was healed when the person should have been consumed by it and died. Bodies of water were split in two when they should have been completely impassible. Food to feed literal thousands was secured from nothing more than a few small fish and a handful of leftover loaves of bread. Massive armies were evaporated without so much as a shot being fired. Dead teenagers were raised to life instead of being dropped in a hole. Paralytic limbs were straightened, and people walked away when they should have crawled away. Oil appeared in jars that were empty, and food fell from the sky. That stuff is all backwards.

The Grand Reversal of The Resurrection

Then there is the grand reversal of the resurrection. It began with an execution reversed, whereby He who was innocent was brutally executed by those who were guilty. It was an inhumane execution turned into ingenious sacrifice, whereby an end for one man turned into a beginning for all men. It was a devout religious leader who should have cast his vote against this man, who instead carried this man's body into his own tomb. Three days later it was an empty tomb when it should not have been, leaving a dead man walking (which is a reversal of the most astounding sort). It was a group of terrified disciples keeping their heads down while crawling back to their old lives, now standing directly in front of the man they watched lose His. It was all backwards.

These were all uncategorically opposite of what should have been. It doesn't get more opposite than that. If we apply the realities of the existence within which each of us are forced to live, these things and so many more were and are completely backwards. They were completely opposite of how it all should work. They simply did not and do not fit into how we have conceptualized the realities of the existence within which we are forced to operate, and how we have concurrently determined the permanently fixed limitations that define our humanity. They are backwards.

Going Forward

To fix this conundrum, might we say that to go forward we must indeed be willing to go backwards.

And I suppose the best way to do that is to switch the two of these in our minds by reversing our perception of how this existence actually operates. And we cannot do that unless we include God, for God is the single and sole thing that reverses the limits of our humanity by quite literally obliterating those limits with His limitlessness. He does not live with the confining rubrics created by our confining thought processes. He is not afraid to step into the impossible, because it will always surrender to Him. His existence is defined by that which is infinite, which means He cannot be defined. Therefore, we must comprehensively trade who we are for what He is, and in the trading trade off everything of us in the exchange.

We must understand that it is not our limits that define our existence at all, although we have foolishly surrendered to that terribly myopic idea. We are not big enough nor powerful enough to define the extent of our existence. Rather, it is God's power and God's nature that defines it. We must understand or at least accept the immense, radical and in many cases incomprehensible difference between who we are and who God is. And out of that understanding we must willingly trade our limitations for God's limitlessness. Indeed, that alone will abruptly turn things around.

A Commitment to Going Backwards

When we do that, backward becomes forward. And when that happens, we will have cut the chains that we've slapped on life. We will have blown out the boundaries that we thought defined us. The 'impossible' now becomes wholly canted toward the 'possible', and the horizons that we had tightly fixed on our lives suddenly blow out to horizons that are horizon-less. It is a radical reorientation that unleashes us from the confines of our own self-imposed prisons. Indeed, going backwards is going forwards.

Standing in the gaping space now created, we suddenly start to understand that dreams are more than hopeful fantasies that our minds toy with. Rather, they become realities that life is changed with. That a vision for something better can move from 'nice idea' to 'transforming ideal'. That hope is not some thin thing that is subject to the winds of fate, but it is crafted hard by the hands of God. That the end of ourselves is where God begins. That the fear of failure is slain cold by success already hot on the way. That a looming mountain is nothing more than a road in disguise, and that the impossible is not an obstacle but an invitation.

Message Delivered

All of this and more happens when we refuse to continue to go backwards. All of this and more is the true forward. This is the incessant and unrelenting message of God throughout history. And it is a message hand delivered by God's Son Jesus with potent impact at the resurrection. It is a message for anyone who will hear it. It is the single and sole message that can turn us from backward to forward. Therefore, be assured that the direction of our lives, the outcome of our existence, and the impact of this book will hinge on what we do with this single message.

Chapter Twenty-Nine
Words for the Times
Speaking God Into the 21st Century

"How much better it is to get wisdom than gold! And to get understanding is to be chosen above silver."
- Proverbs 16:16 (NIV)

"Set your course by the stars, not by the lights of every passing ship."
- Omar N. Bradley

Both the space and the tolerance to speak the truths of God into the mounting chaos of the 21st century seems to be rapidly diminishing. Clearly, there is a formidable wave of mounting dissent that opposes God with an ever-accelerating intensity. And in facing such a foreboding reality, how do we speak the saving truth of the Gospel into our culture in a way that the message can vigorously slice through the very opposition that stands against the very faith that we are articulating? How do we articulate the message of the Gospel in a way that its voice is raised above the clamor that would otherwise smash it silent? How do we speak truth into a culture that is bent on avoiding the truth at all costs?

It's not about changing the message, for the message was handed to us complete in every way. Rather, it's about understanding both the audience and the cultural climate to which we are delivering the message. Subsequently, we must articulate the message to effectively catch the ears and change the hearts of both. J.B. Phillips put it well when he said:

"If their words are to enter men's hearts and bear fruit, they must be the right words shaped cunningly to pass men's defenses and explode silently and effectually within their minds…we have the formidable task of reconciling the Word of truth with the thought-forms of a people estranged from God; interpreting without changing or diluting the essential Word."

In working with the many people that I am privileged to work with, I have wrestled with the means by which to effectively speak to a dying culture that seems to prefer dying. And along the way, I have authored a number of quotes that embody principles and perspectives that have served me well in gaining an ear for the Gospel. I have included a selection of these quotes in this article out of the hope that they might be of service to you as you seek to lift high the Gospel of Jesus Christ in a world that is bent on shutting Him down. I share these with you a part of this book. May they encapsulate a thought or two that you can carry with you on your own journey and share along the way in whatever way seems best given the opportunity.

Words for the Times:

"If I have relegated God to a fantasy born of frightened men ill-suited to face life, I would suggest that this is far more the story of frightened men who wish God to be a fantasy because they are ill-suited to face Him."

"Are we so gleefully enraptured with our own greed

that we think it wise to banish God to the barest fringes of our existence? For I would surmise that if we are that impoverished, we deserve the destruction that such impoverishment will rain upon us. And in the rain, I must tell you that I will not flee to the fringes to which we have banished God in order to find shelter in His embrace. Rather, I will pray Him into the middle of the rain so that all of us will suddenly find ourselves sheltered from the rain that we had created by the God that we had banished. For such is the character of this God."

"When I find a man sold out to God, I have found a rare thing. And I have discovered that God is in the business of creating rare things, of which I someday hope to be one so that I might help you become one as well."

"I have sat in the impossible places that existed leagues beyond the reach of the prose of men, the touch of friends, and the encouragement of family. And in these horribly famished places where hope languished and desperation ruled, I eventually fell to exhaustion and laid my life in the frigid embrace of an awaiting death only to find that instead I had fallen into the warm hands of a loving God. And while these words are the prose of yet another man, the hands that they speak of are not."

"There is no depth that exceeds the reach of the God who is, at this very moment, seeking you out in the holes that you have dug for yourself."

"I can tell you that God has repeatedly 'raised me

up' in the middle of the innumerable situations where 'up' had become a hope lost in the darkness of the places to which I had fallen. And while that is the miracle of my story, it sits waiting to be the reality of yours."

"The only ethics that will effectively guide mankind are those that mankind did not create."

"If Jesus is in the storm, then there is no need for us to be in the boat. Yet, too many Christians spend all of their time wandering around the marina being in neither boat nor storm."

"We might wish to take note of the fact that it is within the impoverishment of our own thinking that we create these innumerable strategies which we brazenly herald as the means to mankind's salvation. And the means by which to halt the incessant travesties that this failed reality repeatedly births is to acknowledge the impoverishment of our relationship with the God who has already secured our salvation."

"How do I come to believe in God? Immerse yourself in the alternatives."

"Mankind is on a mission to free itself from a God whose mission is to free us from ourselves. And if our mission prevails, we won't."

"I have both the violent turbulence of the storm and the quiet promises of God in the storm. And what I must work to remember is that something is not necessarily stronger simply because it's louder."

"It seems that we are not in a state of disbelief regarding the existence of God. Rather, we are in a state of rebellion against His existence. But have we not yet come to understand that in the end, that kind of rebellion is a rebellion against our own existence?"

"More often than not, it's not that we don't believe in God. Rather, it's that we don't want to."

"It is not ignorance that causes me to follow God, nor is it escapism through some rigorously contrived fantasy. Rather, those are the things that keep me from following the world."

"If you deem me as being a fool because I believe in God, I would only have you look around at the chaos and carnage in the world today and ask what kind of fool would believe in men who don't believe in God?"

"Yes, I believe that God cries. For the heart of any true parent is shattered beyond reparation when they have invested their greatest treasures in their children only to have their children recklessly trample upon those riches as if they were the stuff of nothing. And once they've trampled them sufficiently, to then watch them set out on some spurious path wherein the children live out the whole of their lives themselves being trampled. Oh yes, God cries. Yet, it is I who stands on this road with riches forfeited crying not for the poor choices that I've made, but because I am the child who made God cry."

These are words for today. Words that shake the foundations of who we are and what we believe. They are words that compel us to greater things and the abandonment of lesser ideals. They press against the chafing constraints of a deteriorating culture and call the culture to everything it cannot be on its own. These are words that when applied to our lives can transform our thinking and alter our trajectory. These are words for all of us in this time called the 21st century. However, they are for every person in every time.

Chapter Thirty
Conclusion
The Contradictions of the Christian Life

A conclusion presupposes that something has come to a right and proper end because it is wholly proper and entirely right that it ends. The evidence that something has come to a right and proper conclusion is based on the fact that the resources available for that task have been fully spent, and subsequently the goal is completed in and by the expenditure of those resources. It is my hope that I have accomplished such a feat (at least in part) in the writing of this book.

However, too often a conclusion is not based on that reality at all. Rather, we often decide if something's concluded. We often render that judgement. And in rendering those judgements, we often dispose of something while it's still vibrant, robust, and very much alive. And those unfortunate decisions frequently bring about the death of things long before they're actually dead. More tragically, in some cases they bring about the death of something that was never supposed to die at all. With that said, there is much more that can be said than the handful of words penned into the pages of this single book. Nonetheless, we tend to conclude things that maybe shouldn't be concluded. And the broader question might be, "Why do we do that?"

The Purpose of Our Conclusions

As with anything related to our humanity, we do

things for reasons. The reasons themselves may be sound or they may not be sound. Nonetheless, we do things for reasons and we conclude things prematurely for reasons as well. As you venture forward with your life, you may want to make certain that you do not bring to a conclusion the thoughts that this book has generated for you or the inspiration that it may have provided. Growth is life-long. There is no conclusion. And it is the same for our growth in our relationship with God. Therefore, why do we conclude things prematurely? Following are some possible reasons.

Conclusions to Avoid a Battle

By their very nature, conclusions imply that we no longer need to fight for the continuation of something because it's supposed to be over. If something's concluded, we can pull up, catch our breath, wipe our brow in relief, and sneak off a battlefield that we hated being on in the first place. Therefore, if we can call something as concluded, we can conclude our need to fight for it. Avoiding a battle of just about any kind is pretty compelling. Therefore, we often take license and determine that something's concluded because we really don't want to fight the battle anymore. And we therefore find ourselves calling it good in order to prematurely excuse ourselves from a battle that we really don't want any part of.

Conclusions as Avoiding Abandonment

Conclusions also give us permission to abandon something under the guise that whatever it is, it's done. The whole idea of abandonment is rather distasteful for most of us. It implies a rather pathetic cowardice fed by fear that incessantly drives us away from great things and into the shadow of nothing. Far too often fear prevails and cowardice wins the day. But we've rather astutely figured out that we can readily side-step the shame of cowardice by saying that something's done. It's completed. We convince ourselves that we don't need to fight for it because there's nothing left to fight for. By our definition of cowardice, the battle is rightly concluded. And in that decision, we have handed ourselves a ready excuse to flee the battlefield in a manner where we look more the victor than the vanquished.

Conclusions as Avoiding Embarrassment

Conclusions free us from having to stand up and fight when everyone else around us has walked away. In a world populated with spineless individuals bent on feeding their own soured appetites, many critical battles have been blatantly abandoned. Battles are by their very nature sacrificial. They demand a commitment to a cause far larger than any individual person fighting the battle. And if perchance the result is victory, those who fought the battle may not have the privilege of ever experiencing the fruits of that victory. Because of those rather sharp realities, many walk away. And with the ranks embarrassingly depleted, we often seem the fool if we stick around. Yet, if we simply call the battle concluded, we free our conscience to walk off the battlefield with the droves that are walking before us. We save face in the embrace of a lie.

Conclusions as Avoiding Failure

Conclusions free us from the potential awkwardness that we might feel in having attempted to save something only to fail miserably in the effort. We can be brave, and we can be bold. But neither insulate us from potential failure. Conclusions give us the ability to step away from something before we've been in it long enough to fail at it. Despite the fact that it's not concluded, we often walk through this thing we're engaged in, picking out a success here and a success there. And in holding those scrapes up we declare that we've succeeded and that we can close up shop and go home. Or we can dumb-down our goals so the task looks completed. Or we can cite the proverbial escapist clause that 'it's about as good as it gets' and then get going. When we do, we feign victory when we're living defeat.

Conclusions as Focusing on Other Stuff

Sometimes we just want to focus on what we want to focus on. Maybe we think that the world is moving forward without us, or a social group is distancing itself from us, or our career aspirations are not all that inspiring right now. We've hit a slump and what we're doing is not getting us out of the slump. Therefore, we want to get in the saddle, grab hold of the reins, and mosey off to what we think are greener pastures. Conclusions then become the stirring of our agendas and our eventual surrender to them. We sense that "It's high time that we did something for us," which often results in something that's going to damage us. And so, we shut it down.

The Consequence

And because we engage in these behaviors, we bury many things that in reality aren't dead. Our lives are littered with a host of unnecessary graves that hold things that are still very much alive. We've buried opportunity, and we've interred hope. We've closed down relationships, and we've closed out dreams. We've nailed fresh ideas in pine boxes, and we've entombed possibilities that are now rendered impossible for the single and sole reason that we buried them alive. We've scraped the surface, but we missed the treasure underneath (often by mere inches). We've just touched the barest edge of the growth that's available to us, but we've pawned off the opportunity of growth for the lure of lesser things. It is phenomenally tragic that we errantly label something as concluded when the only thing that's concluded is the fact that it's begun.

A Needed Message

Is that not the message of the Gospel? When on a hill framed by three crosses mankind concluded that it was done. When a body was taken down from a cross, wrapped and placed in the finality of a tomb, mankind claimed that it was over. When the grand spectacle concluded and everybody went home to the regularity and routine of their sluggish lives, they went to sleep that night believing that it was over. When everyone thought nothing to be different and that hope was now sealed in history, all of that was about to be unleashed. Everyone determined a beginning as a conclusion. With the lesson of the work of Christ apparently yet unlearned, mankind has far too often carried that suffocating pattern of behavior right into the present leaving our lives and our culture littered with graves filled with things yet very much alive.

The Christian life itself begs us to refrain from killing life before its dead. The life that God grants us declares that our notions of conclusions are nothing more than indicators of beginnings. God invites us to believe that what is done is often only done because we have deemed it so, and that such a judgement does not possess the power to actually make it so. The Christian life is a promise that there is always something that follows the darkest night, the most desolate moment, the most detestable actions, and the most searing pain. Walking with God is about conclusions being the very beginnings that we are in such desperate need of. A relationship with God asks that we quit burying that which is not dead out of the fear of how glorious life might actually be if we let it live. That is both the promise and invitation of the Christian life.

Conclusion

There is too much that has died in our world. There is too much that we have ignorantly (and often purposely) buried. And our lives are the poorer for such misguided actions. This book has been about moving forward. About living in a new way. A fresh way. Even a radical way. It's about an intentional infusion of the principles by which God would have us live. It's about living by those principles so that we can walk in the footsteps of the few. It's living as Jesus lived and walking in a manner bold, sometimes outrageous, perpetually liberating, but always Godly and thoughtful. It is about the narrow way, for that is the only way.

We need men and women who live out their lives in

that manner. Men and women who realize that there is no conclusion to such a walk. Rather, there is a commitment that stretches beyond this troubled existence of ours into the halls and haven of heaven. Therefore, it is my hope that your walk with God will never be upended by a conclusion of any kind, and that you will strive to live out what Jesus died to give you. May your journey be blessed. May it be rich. May it take you to the highest of places and grant you the grandest of vistas. Indeed, may you be blessed and may other be blessed as you walk in the footsteps of the few by living out a truly principled life.